Raising

YOUR CHILDREN'S

Children

Help for Grandparents Raising Grandkids

MARTHA EVANS SPARKS

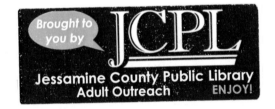

BEACON HILL PRESS

OF KANSAS CITY

Copyright 2011
by Martha Evans Sparks and Beacon Hill Press of Kansas City

ISBN 978-0-8341-2563-6

Printed in the
United States of America

Cover Design: Arthur Cherry
Internal Design: Sharon Page

Library of Congress Cataloging-in-Publication Data

Sparks, Martha Evans, 1927-
    Raising your children's children : help for grandparents raising grandkids / Martha Evans Sparks.
        p. cm.
    Includes bibliographical references.
    ISBN 978-0-8341-2563-6 (pbk.)
    1. Grandparents as parents. 2. Grandparent and child. 3. Grandparent and child—Religious aspects—Christianity. 4. Child rearing—Religious aspects—Christianity. I. Title.
    HQ759.9.S69 2011
    248.8'45—dc22

                                                                    2010041752

10 9 8 7 6 5 4 3 2 1

CONTENTS

INTRODUCTION

Feeling guilty, cheated of your retirement, like a failure as a parent, maybe even embarrassed? Or maybe you're reeling from grief over the loss of your own child. Whatever your particular situation, you find yourself cartwheeled into a situation with little warning and needing answers to a lot of questions you never thought you would be asking.

Some grandparents hire lawyers to go to the authorities to try to gain custody of their grandchildren because, as they see it, the parents aren't doing a good job. Maybe they don't like the in-law, or the parents aren't taking the kids to church or allowing the children to stay all night at Grandma's house as often as she would like. These kids are not being abused or exploited. They are being raised responsibly and are as safe as possible. Nevertheless, a jealous or unreasonable grandparent wants custody because things are not being done his or her way. David Godfrey, former managing attorney for the Access to Justice Foundation in Lexington, Kentucky, says that eighty percent of the calls he received from grandparents were of this kind.

This book is for the other twenty percent. For whatever reason, you're raising your grandchild. Your own child may be an addict, in jail, mentally ill, or may have died as a result of disease or accident. Regardless, you're suddenly parenting again.

If you're such a grandparent and you feel overwhelmed physically, emotionally, and financially, read on. Let this book get you headed in the right direction with brief but accurate answers to the most common quandaries grandparents raising grandchildren face.

If you're a pastor or counselor ministering to seniors or a social worker whose job it is to deal with grandparents who are second-time-around parents, you, too, will find basic, accurate, short answers to frequently voiced questions. The answers in this book to legal, physical, and behavioral problems are general in nature, because each of the fifty United States has its own court system and laws. What you will find here is practical advice and information from a Christian viewpoint.

Life may be different than you planned, but it can be good, and you're not alone.

one

PARENTING AGAIN, LIKE IT OR NOT

Alice first met Jacob at 3:00 o'clock one Saturday morning when a woman she had never seen before pounded on her front door. The woman said her name was Mary and that the father of the child standing next to her was Alice's son. Alice hadn't even known of the child's existence.

Jacob looked as if he might be around four years old; he was dirty, silent, and too thin. He had nothing with him but the worn-out clothes he had on. Alice could see her son sitting in the driver's seat of the old car, door open, motor running. He waved half-heartedly. *Lewis is out of jail again,* she thought. Mary asked Alice if she would watch Jacob for a while, and Alice said she supposed so. Mary pushed Jacob through the door, ran back to the car, and Mary and Lewis rattled off into the dark.

What Alice had just experienced is called a *drop-off.* She became one of the six and a half million grandparents in the United States who find themselves with full parental responsibility for their grandchildren. Instead of cuddling them and spoiling them and returning them to their parents, these grandparents must become parents again.

In the United States, seventy-one percent of these grandparents are under the age of sixty.[1] Some of them, though, are older and have retired. With the unexpected mouths to feed and clothing to buy, they must reenter the workforce. In this country, nineteen percent of second-time-around parents and their grandchildren live below the poverty level.

One of the common routes for grandparents to become parents again is when a social worker from an agency such as the Department of Social Services or the Cabinet for Health and Family Services—whatever it's called in a particular state—comes calling. He or she tells the grandparents that the state has removed the child or children from the parental home. The most common reason for this course of action is that the parents have been charged with various crimes connected to alcohol and drugs in addition to neglect, abuse, or abandonment. State agencies prefer to place children with a relative. If they have the name of the grandparents of the child, they will make contact with them and ask if they're willing to take the child and raise him or her, taking full parental responsibility. They are told that if no relative is willing to take the child, he or she will be placed in a foster home.

The second common route for grandparents becoming parents again is family intervention. Perhaps they discover their teenage daughter is pregnant, and they know she's not ready to be a parent. Maybe the dad is a teenager or an older guy who is long gone. Out of concern for the baby and love for their child, they take on the responsibility of bringing the baby into their home. The authorities are never involved, and at the time the grandparents think that's the best idea.

A third common way grandparents become parents is some version of what happened to Alice. Somebody drops the child or children on the doorstep without warning. A typical circumstance is that the person's son or daughter stops by the house with the child and asks the grandparent to watch the baby for a few hours—but the child's biological parent simply never returns.[2]

The situation of grandparents raising grandchildren is approaching epidemic levels in the United States. Eight percent of children under the age of eighteen live with grandparents, a thirty-percent increase between 1990 and 2000. Between eighty and ninety percent of these cases occur because the children's parents are addicted to drugs and/or alcohol.[3]

All socioeconomic levels suffer from abuse and addiction. The impression that it's more prevalent in lower-income groups may grow from the inability of lower-income people to get needed services as quickly as persons with more social and financial resources. Persons with higher incomes are more likely to have support systems in place to help them before the situation becomes uncontrollable. They can hire lawyers or other professionals to rescue the grandchildren before emotional and perhaps physical damage is done by the chaotic lifestyle of drug-addicted parents.[4]

When Alice found herself with a four-year-old boy to raise, she considered her options. She was furious with Lewis for being up to his old tricks and his pattern of thinking only of himself. She knew that her inconvenience—much less Jacob's welfare—never entered Lewis's head. Her first inclination was to pick up the phone and get her son and his child out of her life once and for all. She was sixty-five years old, widowed, short on money, and short on energy. She could call the Department of Social Services (DSS), and a social worker would come and get Jacob and place him in foster care.

But that morning as she stood in the predawn chill, Alice's mental calendar rolled back. She could see Lewis standing in that same spot, looking very much like Jacob. The little boy's big brown eyes and shock of curly hair convinced Alice that he was indeed her son's child. *Am I really prepared to send away my own grandchild— my own flesh and blood—and let him grow up with strangers as a ward of the state? Will he be happy if I do that? Will he end up with people who will be good to him? Will anyone tell him about his birth family?* For all his sins, Lewis was still her son, and she loved him. Even though it was against her better judgment, Alice knew she would keep Jacob. She would stretch her tiny pension as far as it would go. She would take him in, and she would love him.

There was another reason Alice didn't want to make that call: it could cause big trouble for Mary and Lewis. Knowing Lewis's history of substance abuse, Alice surmised that he and his girlfriend were both using drugs and alcohol and almost certainly living in their car. Her call would not only bring Jacob to the attention of the DSS but also Mary and Lewis. In fact, Alice wondered if the reason they had dropped Jacob off with her was that they had reason to believe they were just one step ahead of the authorities. If Jacob was not in their custody when Social Services caught up with them, they might escape charges of neglect, abandonment, and maybe abuse being added to the charges of illegal drug use. Did she want to be responsible for causing them even more trouble than they already had? Conflicted, she argued with herself and lost. She did not make the call.

Alice's situation is a little different from what's known as *kinship care.* This is the term often used to describe the circumstance in which the state removes children from their parents' home because of abuse or neglect or for other reasons. The state looks for relatives, usually grandparents, and after a determination that placement with a relative rather than a non-relative is in the best interest of the child, places the children with grandparents or other relatives. These relatives act as foster parents just as if they were unrelated foster parents, strangers to the child and his or her family. As is usual in such an arrangement, the children remain wards of the state, and the state has the final word in decisions regarding the children.[5]

Alice's life had clearly been turned upside down. A shudder of guilt ran through her. *How did it come to this? How could I mess up my son so badly that now I have to raise my own grandchild? Who will help me? Which way do I turn?*

She knew the first thing to do was to comfort the uprooted child. Alice wondered how it would feel to be four years old and awakened in the night, taken to an unfamiliar place, and left with a stranger.

Jacob stood in silence when Alice offered him a glass of milk. He finally drank it after she convinced him that it was for him and that it was okay to drink all of it. He let her give him a bath. He was still silent next day when they went to buy clothes for him to wear. Alice used the money she was saving for new shoes.

After caring for the child's most immediate needs, grandparents who find themselves in this situation should do several things.

Establish Paternity

It's a good idea to establish the identity of both parents rather than just making sure that the child belongs to your child. If you can find a birth certificate, it should list the mother. It may or may not list the father, and certainly it won't list grandparents. The supposed father's name on the birth certificate is not enough to establish paternity.[6]

Think Long-Term

Be realistic about the duration of this life adjustment. Grandparents often believe that their son or daughter just needs to work through this tough period before coming back for the child or children. "All I want is for my daughter to get her life straightened out and get her children back. I realize she has problems, but surely when she sees she's lost her children, she'll be motivated to turn her life around."

Grandparents tend to convince themselves that their son or daughter will get it together in a few months and return for the child. This line of thinking is almost always a mistake. It's unrealistic to think in terms of raising the child or children for months rather than years. If the parents can eventually take their children back, you can be pleasantly surprised. But don't count on it happening soon; it may never happen. Formalize some kind of custody arrangement immediately. We'll go into this in more detail in chapter two.

No matter how hard it is to face, assume that you're in this for a long time, maybe until the child becomes an adult. Make legally enforceable plans for someone to care for the child if you should become incapacitated. This is covered in an upcoming chapter.

Circuit Court Judge JoAnn Wise of the Fayette County, Kentucky, Family Court says, "Never ever when the [government] has become involved sit back and see what happens. If government agencies have become involved, in practical terms within a year those children may be given to somebody else. . . . Waiting back when [government] is involved is very, very dangerous. You should never sit back." Judge Wise makes the point that the people who tend to get their children back are the ones who have the support of their families.

"The [government] loves to know . . . they have somebody else . . . there to be their eyes and ears. And if they know they have the family support and . . . they know the grandparents are going to step in and do something when needed, that goes a long way to get kids back. . . . It's the parents who don't seem to have any family support who lose out."

Quit Worrying About Alienating the Child's Parents

The parents have bombed out, or you wouldn't be in this position. Of course, you still love your wayward child. Of course, you're embarrassed and maybe angry at the effect his or her actions are having on the family. But your focus must be on what's good for the child and on preserving your own health and sanity. What should be your child's responsibility is now yours. Call the authorities yourself. Say something such as "I want to help my grandchild, but my resources are limited. I need to establish paternity, and I need to get custody and make long-term plans. What can I do? Can you help me?" Be sure to get the name of the person with whom you talk.

This will bring your child and the other parent to the attention of the authorities. It may mean that charges will be filed against the other parent. It may mean that you'll have to say to your child, "I'll do what I can to help you straighten out your life, and I'll emotionally support you. But I will not do it to the detriment of the child. So if the situation warrants it, I will step up and become your adversary to protect the child."

Contact a Lawyer Who Specializes in Family Law

At some point most grandparents who become parents again need professional legal help to negotiate the legal system. Only a member of the bar can go into court and file a motion, which is a formal request of the court to get something done. You will need a lawyer to help you gain custody of your grandchild. This is necessary so that you can enroll the child in school and make medical decisions and other important decisions on the child's behalf. Legally enforceable plans must be made to care for the child if your health fails or you die. Otherwise, there's a risk that your grandchild will be placed with strangers or returned to unfit parents. A lawyer can also help you find out what if any financial assistance is available to you from your state. And having legal representation is important if you have to fend off efforts from your own child to take your grandchild back into a bad living situation.

If you're not in a position to pay for a lawyer, there are several options. Call the local bar association and explain that you need legal help and cannot afford to pay the full fee. The bar association will have a list of lawyers who do *pro bono*—in other words free—legal work. In addition, the bar association can provide you with names of lawyers who will work for reduced fees to serve those of limited income. Another option is to look in the white pages of your local telephone book under "Legal Aid" or on the Internet using "legal aid" as the search term. You'll find links to legal aid offices in your area. Legal aid lawyers will help you at little or no cost. The Yellow Pages may have an entry called "Legal Services" with helpful numbers.

If you have trouble locating a legal aid program in your area, look in the section of the telephone book for the state office listings. Some states have a toll-free help line for older adults, or you may find an entry for "Senior Citizens Center" or "Area Agency on Aging" or a similar name. Such an agency can direct you to help. If worse comes to worse, call a local lawyer. Whoever answers the phone should be able to give you information about local legal aid services.

Find a Support Group

You're not alone—support groups are everywhere. Find one and join it. If you have a church, share your situation with those friends. Find and talk with other grandparents who are raising their grandchildren. If you speak with someone at a government agency—a social worker, perhaps—he or she may know of local support groups. And once again, remember: you're not alone.

Remember: nothing takes God by surprise.

Lord, help me be equal to this task.
It seems too big right now.

Questions for Support Group Discussion

1. How did you come to be raising your children's children?

2. Have you established your grandchild's paternity?

3. Of the things mentioned in this chapter that should be done quickly, talk about which if any have been accomplished by the members of your group.

4. Do you worry about your relationship with your own child now that you're raising his or her child?

5. If some members of your group have been in contact with a lawyer concerning custody issues, ask them to talk about that.

6. How many in your group feel they're delaying making long-term decisions about raising their grandchildren?

two

WHAT IS LEGAL CUSTODY?

When Carolyn gets to drinking, her five-year-old daughter, Hallie, usually goes to the back bedroom and stays there. But on this particular day, when Hallie's dad—Carolyn's boyfriend, Johnny—came home unexpectedly, the fighting was louder than usual. Hallie peeked out just in time to see her mother throw a water pitcher at Johnny. The man ducked, and the glass pitcher smashed into the wall. Carolyn went after Johnny with a chunk of the broken glass.

Little Hallie called 911.

When the policeman came to the door, Johnny pushed Carolyn into the bedroom with Hallie and smilingly assured the policeman that it was only a minor domestic squabble and that Hallie had overreacted.

After the policeman left, Carolyn rounded on her daughter.

"If you ever do that again, they'll come and take you away, and you'll never get to see mom and dad again."

"Where will they take me?"

"Far away."

Even though Carolyn and Johnny are heroin addicts, they're not stupid. They knew that little Hallie's call, noted by the 911 operator as a "domestic disturbance," could trigger an investigation of their home. Carolyn was telling Hallie the truth: if the facts of

Hallie's home life were uncovered, Hallie could be removed from the only home she had ever known.

Governmental agencies learn by several routes about children who may be living with unfit parents. In many cities, any domestic disturbance call like the one Hallie made automatically triggers a petition to the local social services agency. Someone, maybe a police officer or a social worker, goes to the address and checks for evidence of child neglect or abuse.

The agencies responsible for determining the abuse or neglect of children are called different things in different states. In your state it may be called Department of Social Services, Family Services Agency, Department of Children and Families, Cabinet for Health and Family Services, or something similar to these.

Although it varies, in some jurisdictions anytime a police officer makes an arrest for any reason, if it's discovered that the person arrested is a parent, it sets off an investigation of the status of any young children who may be in the care of the arrested person.

Abused, neglected, or even abandoned children also come to the attention of authorities through anonymous phone calls, often from a neighbor or even a friend of the family.

Many hospitals routinely perform drug tests on all women who deliver babies in that hospital. If the mother tests positive for illegal drugs, her newborn is removed from her custody and placed in foster care by the state.

Regardless of how a child comes to the attention of the state, if the child is removed from his or her natural parents, the child is placed in a foster home while authorities attempt to find relatives who will take the child. The child will be sent for long-term foster care with strangers only if no grandparent, aunt, uncle, or other relative can be found who's willing and able to take the child.

As it turned out, it was Carolyn and Johnny who put distance between themselves and their little girl. Not long after Hallie's call to 911, they dropped her off with Johnny's sister, also a heroin user.

Nobody paid attention to Hallie's sobs and pleas not to be separated from the adults who provided the only shred of stability she had ever known.

When Sandy, Carolyn's mother, heard about Hallie's circumstances, she rescued the child. That was three years ago. Sandy and her husband, Wallace, were already raising Carolyn's and Johnny's oldest child, Patrick.

"Where are Carolyn and Johnny now?" I asked Sandy.

"Out of state, we think," she replied. "It's been almost a year since we heard from them."

Hallie, now eight years old, has trouble sleeping. Her grandmother believes it's because of the child's conflicted state of mind. "She misses her mommy, yet thinking of her makes her nervous. She keeps asking me, 'Granny, are they going to send me far away?'"

"I say, 'No, baby, nobody's going to take you away from your Granny.' But am I telling her the truth? What if Carolyn and Johnny show up? They're Hallie's and Patrick's blood kin, natural parents. Can I stop them from taking the kids? Carolyn is my daughter, and I still love her. But let her try to raise these children? No way."

Hallie's brother Patrick is thirteen now. He has anxiety attacks that his grandmother believes are caused by his fear that his parents will appear out of the blue and claim him. "This is my home now," Patrick says, waving an arm toward his grandparents' house.

Sandy Crane is a supervisor for a crew of cleaning women at a local nursing home. She works from 7 A.M. until 3:30 P.M. five days a week. She's forty-nine years old. She manages to attend all of Patrick's ball games, and she takes him to karate lessons every Friday. On Saturday mornings she drives Hallie to ballet class, which Hallie loves.

Sandy's husband, Wallace Crane, is a master electrician. Patrick was born to their daughter, Carolyn, when she was sixteen.

Johnny, Patrick's father, was seventeen at the time and was as unprepared as Carolyn to be a parent. Patrick has lived with his grandparents his whole life. Wallace, who is fifty years old, had planned to retire soon. Then came the added responsibility of Hallie. Forget retirement.

"Wallace works in another state," Sandy said when I asked if taking in the kids put stress on their marriage. "Wallace doesn't have a lot of patience. The kids get on his nerves. He says he used up all his tolerance on our first set of children." Sandy thinks he works out of state because he's tired of raising kids. He sends money home regularly to help support his grandchildren, and he comes home for a few days about every three months. Sandy took the grandchildren to Louisiana to visit him once.

Sandy's biggest fears are the same as the children's: what if something happens to her and Wallace, and what if Carolyn and Johnny show up and want the kids back? It also bothers her and Wallace that although they think they don't have the legal right to do so, they've made decisions for their grandchildren. When Hallie had an earache, they took her to their doctor and gave her the medication the physician prescribed. Did they have the legal right to decide on medical treatment for her? Sandy isn't sure. As informal caregivers without an official legal relationship, Sandy says there were many difficulties to iron out when she enrolled the children in school. Patrick enjoys playing soccer, but they're afraid that if he gets hurt, they would be held accountable for allowing an extracurricular activity involving risk when they had no legal right to make decisions for the children.

Making It Legal

If you're making a home for your grandchildren, your first action after establishing paternity should be to obtain formal custody.

Two general types of custody exist: physical custody and legal custody. Physical custody is when a grandparent takes care of a child without a court order to do so. That's the kind of custody Sandy and Wallace Crane have of their grandchildren. Physical custody refers to where the child lives, eats, and sleeps, but it does not grant legal rights.[1]

Legal custody is obtained when a judge in a court of law gives the grandparent—or another adult who is not a natural parent—the legal right to take care of the child. Lawyer David Godfrey says, "A grandparent who wants legal custody has to go to court and prove to the judge that it is in the best interest of the child for someone other than the birth parents to have custody."[2] He adds that when grandparents have legal custody, the birth parents will have to go to court to get their children back. They can't just knock on the door and demand them.

Legal custody gives the grandparent or other adult the legal right to care for the child, including making medical and educational decisions. If you have legal custody, you can decide where the child lives. You have the right to make decisions concerning sports that may carry a risk of injury. A court order of guardianship or custody will generally say that you can make health care decisions for the child. You should take a copy of the court order to the health care provider when you take your grandchild in for care.

If you have legal custody of your grandchild and have group health insurance through your employer, you can probably add the child to your policy. If you carry health insurance on an individual policy, the insurance company may add the child to your policy only if you have legal custody. You may find that purchasing a separate policy for the child alone is no more expensive than adding him or her to an existing policy.[3]

Depending on your income level, your household may be eligible for Medicaid, the government's health insurance program for persons with low income. If you apply for Medicaid for your grandchild only, he or she would still be considered part of your household, and your income and savings would be counted in determining eligibility for Medicaid.[4] Medicare, the health insurance plan for older adults, is an individual policy, and you cannot add anyone to your Medicare coverage.

State laws vary. What follows is *general* information. The details of laws of the state you live in may be different.

Some states have what is called *de facto* custody laws that allow grandparents or other adults to get legal custody of a child by showing that they have been the child's *de facto* custodian.[5] *De facto* is a Latin term meaning "in fact." In this instance, it means that the person asking to be named custodian is in charge of the children *in fact.* Your state may not call it *de facto* custody, but it may have laws with a similar effect. You will need a lawyer, preferably one who specializes in family law, to present your case. The court will determine from the evidence whether you qualify as the *de facto* custodian of the children. No matter whose legal responsibility it is to take care of these children, are you, the grandparent, in fact providing physical and financial care for them?

As pointed out in the first chapter, if you can't afford a lawyer, call your city or state's bar association for a list of lawyers who do *pro bono* work or search out legal aid, who can help you at little or no cost.

Your state will likely ask you to prove that you are in fact the custodian for these children by showing clear and convincing evidence that you, the person or persons petitioning to be named *de facto* custodian, have been the primary caregiver and have provided financial support of a child residing with you—

- For six months or more if the child is less than three years of age.
- For a year or more if the child is three years of age or older. The time and age requirements may differ state to state.

If the court is convinced that the person petitioning has presented the high standard of evidence necessary to be named a *de facto* custodian, then this places the *de facto* custodian on the same footing as the biological parents when the court is deciding what is in the child's best interests. It levels the playing field between the biological parents and non-parents whether the non-parents are grandparents, aunts, uncles, or even unrelated persons who have taken in a child needing care.

"This is a tremendous result for non-parents," says lawyer Carl Devine, who practices family law in Lexington, Kentucky. "If you are designated a *de facto* custodian, it means you have the same rights as a biological parent, meaning that the biological parent no longer has the preference, no longer has the upper hand. It means the court will look at the *de facto* custodian and the biological parent and give them the same weight in determining what is in the best interest of that child."[6]

Grandparents may strengthen their case to be appointed custodian by having available for the judge's inspection receipts or other proof of payment of the child's expenses. Keep track of what you spend for clothing for the child, for school expenses of all kinds, for doctor and other medical bills, and for other expenditures made especially for the child. Prove to the court in these practical ways that you're providing for the child or children.

"Permanent custody" is another term you'll hear. Sometimes when a governmental agency removes a child from a home deemed unfit because of abuse, abandonment, or neglect, the court will give the natural parents a specific amount of time to work through a "case plan" the government authorities set up for them. This could include things like getting and holding a regular job, having a place to live (other than an automobile), and proving they're off drugs or alcohol. In other words, the parents are given a timeframe in which to get their act together and prove they will be adequate parents.

If the parents do not make changes for the better and "work the case plan" in the time allotted, the state may close the case and award permanent custody to whoever has the child at the time the case comes before the court. This is why, as pointed out earlier, grandparents or other relatives who want the child should make an attempt to gain custody early on. If they hesitate, they may lose the child altogether.

If the Cranes had a permanent custody order in place, it would be extremely difficult for the natural parents to regain custody of their children. They can try, of course, but they must go through the court, and it's not an easy thing to accomplish. Such a custody order would put to rest the kind of fears that bedevil Hallie and Patrick, who live in dread of their parents snatching them away from their grandparents' home.

Occasionally, if everybody agrees on everything, you can settle custody matters on your own. But you probably will need someone licensed to practice law to file a motion with a judge concerning the matter.

The judge—also referred to as *the court*—will always attempt to do what is in the best interests of the child or children. Ideally this would be for the child to live with both his or her natural—or biological—parents. When that is not possible, a judge must decide what the next-best thing is. What the law requires a judge to consider in determining custody varies from state to state but will typically include the following:

- The wishes of the child's parents and any *de facto* custodian. Remember: if the grandparents or other concerned persons have been formally named *de facto* custodians by the court, their wishes will be considered equally with those of the biological parents.
- The wishes of the child if he or she is old enough to speak on his or her own behalf.

- The interaction of the child with his or her parent or parents, siblings, and others who might affect the child's best interests.
- How well is the child adjusted to his or her home, school, and community?
- The mental and physical health of all individuals involved.
- Is there evidence of domestic violence?
- The extent to which the child has been nurtured and emotionally supported by the *de facto* custodian.
- If the biological parents are placing the child with a *de facto* custodian, why are they doing this?
- If the biological parents are now seeking custody, were they prevented from doing so before because of domestic violence in their relationship with each other? Did the state intervene in the past because these parents were charged with neglect or abuse of the child, or was the child placed with a *de facto* custodian in the past in order to allow the parent now seeking custody to work or attend school?
- Has the biological parent just been released from jail and is now seeking the return of children to his or her custody?[7]

Getting *de facto* custody or permanent custody of a child does not mean grandparents are home free. It means only that you, as grandparents, are on an equal footing with the parents. Your standing before the court is equal with that of the biological parents. This means the court will listen to what you have to say. Once you're declared a *de facto* custodian, your voice regarding the child's rights cannot be silenced. You are then in a position to move ahead to the next step and ask the court for permanent legal custody of your grandchildren. Legal custody, remember, is when you as a grandparent have the legal right to care for the child.

Another term you'll hear is "guardianship," which is easier to get than custody. Guardianship and legal custody are similar because both are ordered by a court and give the legal right to make decisions for the child. The rights of the parents do not end when a grandparent or other relative is appointed the guardian of their child. In fact, the natural parents are still responsible for financial support of the child. However, the natural parents cannot take the child from the guardian without a court hearing to end the guardianship. The guardian's duties end when the child becomes eighteen years old or marries, even if he or she is younger than eighteen when the marriage takes place.

Among the reasons grandparents may ask a court to be appointed legal guardians of a grandchild are

- The child's parents are unable to provide a safe and stable home.
- The parents are dead, missing, in jail, or addicted to drugs.
- The parents are abusing the child.
- To have authority to make medical or educational decisions.
- The parents are going to be gone temporarily for military service, or perhaps for an educational opportunity out of the country.[8]

Is there a way to gain custody of a child without the birth parents' consent? Yes, but people hesitate to use it because it can tear a family apart. Suppose five-year-old Hallie had continued to live with her natural parents, Carolyn and Johnny. Then suppose that her grandparents, Sandy and Wallace, fear for the child's safety if she continues to live in an environment of drugs and alcohol and her parents refuse to let her live with her grandparents. The grandparents will have to go to court to get custody. To have Hallie removed from her parents' home, her grandparents must prove to the judge's satisfaction that the biological parents are unfit or have waived their superior right to custody of the child. Such situations are sometimes termed "extraordinary circumstances" and will have an influence on the judge's decision on custody. The child's best interest is always the primary consideration as far as the judge can learn it. Situations like the following would be included:

- Mental illness that renders the parent unable to care for the child.
- Acts of abuse or neglect; for example, the child is malnourished and dirty.
- Alcohol or drug abuse.
- Domestic violence.
- Any crime by a parent that leads to the death or physical or mental disability of a member of the household.
- If a court has appointed a guardian for the parent because of the parent's disability.

People hesitate to put such a proceeding into motion because proving hurtful things in open court against other family members may end any further relationship with them. In this case it would be your grandchild's parents, who, of course, would include your own child.[9]

These are some of the issues in gaining custody of your grandchildren. The only way to be certain of having your grandchildren's placement with you unchallenged forever is to adopt them. Adoption itself raises other issues, which are discussed in Chapter 3.

Our laws are designed to protect the weak.

Father, give me the wisdom to make good decisions for this child who needs me.

Questions for Support Group Discussion

1. There are several ways children come to the attention of the authorities. If your grandchild was placed in your home at the request of authorities, discuss how that came about.

2. Do you feel you have a good grasp on which type of custody arrangement would work best for you?

3. Discuss how different ones in your group arrived at their decisions about which custody arrangement to pursue.

4. Discuss the "extraordinary circumstances" that might persuade a court to give grandparents custody against the wishes of the child's natural parents, and ask for input from anyone in your group who has experienced or expects to experience that.

three

THE PROS AND CONS OF ADOPTING GRANDCHILDREN

The day after Sally learned that her eldest daughter had a life-threatening genetic heart defect, her middle child, twenty-two-year-old Allyn, announced she was pregnant, and the FBI wanted her boyfriend, Charlie, for parole violations.

"After I picked myself up off the floor and quit yelling at her," Sally said, "I told her, 'You get yourselves down to the courthouse and find some judge or magistrate or somebody to marry you. Then go see the FBI. In that order. Now—get this mess cleared up.'"

"Where did she meet Charlie?" I asked.

"In a bar. She was 21 at the time, about to begin her last year of college. We wanted her to finish her education before she married. Instead, she dropped out of school and moved in with Charlie. So I was doing the mother-of-the-bride thing, thinking a small wedding at the country club. Then she comes home with this outrage.

"When Allyn and Charlie first talked of getting married," continued Sally, "my husband, Ed, and I kept trying to find out something about Charlie, but we were never able to find out anything. We understand now why he was vague about his work history. We discovered too late that he had served jail time for all sorts of drug violations—possession, using, selling. You name it—he had done it. The court paroled him, but he couldn't stay clean and drug-free."

Sally and her husband both grew up in the state where Ed now practices law. Three daughters were born to them, Donna, Allyn, and Jennifer. Ed's law practice flourished. As the girls got older, Sally became her husband's office manager.

Donna and Jennifer sailed through college, married suitable men, and each settled into her own happy family life. Allyn was cut from another pattern.

Following Sally's ultimatum, Allyn and Charlie married. He turned himself in and served two more years in jail, fulfilling his sentence. While he was in jail, the Arnolds let Allyn live with them. She quit using drugs while she was pregnant. As soon as her little girl, whom she named Cody, was born, she returned to crack cocaine. Her parents paid for treatment at three different rehab facilities, none of them successful. Alarmed at the prospect of their granddaughter growing up in the slapdash care of a drug-addicted mother, Allyn's parents began proceedings to obtain legal custody of Cody.

It was not a smooth ride. When Charlie got out of jail, the couple moved in with his parents, Marcus and Rebecca, taking Cody with them. Charlie's father is an automobile mechanic. His wife, Rebecca, Charlie's mother, is bipolar and has never worked outside the home. Charlie is their only child.

While living with Charlie's parents, Allyn and Charlie began to disappear, sometimes for a week at a time. They left Cody with her grandmother, Rebecca, who evidently was not bothered by the unexplained absences of her son and daughter-in-law. She never called Sally and Ed to report their mysterious disappearances.

Then one day Allyn dropped Cody off with her parents. "Charlie's gotten physically abusive," she said. "I'm going to Georgia for a while."

"That's all the notice we got of having another child to raise," said Sally. "So much for her taking responsibility for her child. We heard nothing from her. That's when I got on a real personal basis with the police department in Savannah, Georgia."

Allyn lived on the streets of Savannah for several years. Her parents eventually quit trying to rescue their daughter. They realized they could not help her.

Instead of continuing to press for legal custody, Sally and Ed began official moves toward adopting Cody. Because they were blood-kin relatives, the process was longer and more frustrating than if they had been adopting a child who was a stranger to them. First they had to obtain, through legal procedures, an "agreed order" from the parents—Allyn and Charlie—to give them temporary custody of Cody, who was by then two years old. From that point a year had to elapse before they could request permanent custody, which included having the child's birth parents deemed unfit. That required another one-year waiting period. Finally, with the help of their lawyer, Allyn's and Charlie's parental rights were terminated, and Ed and Sally were able to adopt Cody.

Adoption laws vary from state to state. However, some of the concerns that must be addressed are the same in every state.

Adoption, unlike any other form of custody, means that the child becomes the adoptive parents' own child, just as if he or she had been born to them. The child's natural parents—both the mother and father—give up their parental rights forever. This is true even if the biological father and biological mother were never married. This is called termination of parental rights.

When a child is adopted through an agency, the agency has more than likely already obtained from the biological parents a legal agreement to terminate parental rights. But when a relative adopts a child from a family member, the process can be longer, as Sally and Ed discovered.

What are some of the reasons grandparents choose to formally adopt one or more of their grandchildren?

- If the child has been legally adopted, the natural parents cannot appear without warning and demand the child back.

This is often the reason grandparents pursue adoption. As explained earlier, if grandparents or others who have been taking care of the child have legal custody, it prevents the biological parents—who may be virtual strangers to the child—from taking him or her without warning. There must at least be a court hearing first. But the court may allow the biological parent or parents to take the child. More than one toddler has been carried screaming from his or her grandparents' home with little warning because the grandparents lost the custody battle. In this case there is no legal way to permanently prevent the natural parents from taking the child.

If the child has been adopted, however, there is no longer room for legal maneuvering. The child belongs to his or her adoptive parents, just as if he or she had been born to them.

- If the child is legally adopted, the grandparents can make provisions for the child if they become unable to care for the child.

Sally said, "If something happens to Ed and me before Cody is grown and on her own, we have the legal papers in place for her to go to our oldest daughter, Donna. It gives us great peace of mind."

"If we had not adopted," said Sally, "and we should die or be incapacitated, we could not have specified who would raise Cody. More than likely her father's parents would take her. We didn't want that to happen, not only because Rebecca is bipolar and may be unable to care for herself, much less a young child, but because they are almost as old as Ed and I are and might not live much longer than us." Sally hesitates. "Another reason is that their values are different from ours." They don't believe the other grandparents would encourage Cody to go to college.

- It may be financially wiser to adopt.

If a parent has a minor child, adopted or natural, then the parent becomes eligible for Social Security at age sixty-two. If that child is unmarried and under eighteen, or eighteen but still in high school, or any age and is disabled before age twenty-two, he or she becomes eligible for Social Security payments.[1]

Many grandparents will turn sixty-two years of age and become eligible for Social Security payments before the grandchild they adopted is eighteen. Keep in mind that Social Security rules change frequently and are complex. These laws can change, so it's wise to check with the Social Security office. There are some financial helps, however, that will be lost if an adoption takes place. This is discussed later in this chapter.

• If the child is adopted, it creates not only physical permanence but also mental and emotional stability for the child.

Many children who wind up living with grandparents are emotionally scarred from abuse or neglect. They've watched Dad beat up Mom and wondered, *Will I be next?* They've gone hungry because their parents were high on drugs or passed-out drunk. Often these children have moved many times because their parents lived in a car or parked the child with a friend or relative for some period of time. The child has never bonded with anyone, suffering from what psychologists call attachment disorders, which will be discussed in a future chapter. Once he or she is adopted, the procession of strange adults coming and going in the child's life will end. The child can be assured the adoptive parents will be calling the shots from now on.

At first, kids like Cody are skeptical.

"When we first got Cody permanently," Sally says, "we lost some friends, because we just couldn't go out socially for a while. Cody was six years old and absolutely did not want us out of her sight. Her separation anxiety was so great that we felt it would be destructive to her emotionally to be left with a babysitter. Now that she's older, Cody understands that when we go out for an evening, we'll come back. Our absence does not mean that we're passing her along to another stranger."

Although Cody has relaxed considerably and her confidence in her adoptive parents has increased, Sally and Ed still believe it's not wise to leave Cody, who is now ten years old, with a sitter very often.

- Adoption simplifies relationships with schools, doctors, and other professionals in the child's life.

When Sally and Ed adopted Cody, her last name was changed to their last name. As adoptive parents, they can make medical and educational decisions for Cody without being challenged.

- It ends the hassle and worry of when or if the biological parent or parents will show up to reclaim the child and expose the child to danger or neglect.

The grandparents customarily continue to hope that the child's biological parents will straighten out their lives, get off drugs or alcohol, and become responsible for parenting their own child. But what if they've failed in rehab programs, are unpredictably in and out of their child's life, and present a continuing threat to the child's well-being and peace of mind? It may be time to seek to have the parents' rights terminated.

As already noted, it's necessary to have the parental rights of the biological parents terminated in order to adopt the child. When the birth parents sign the papers agreeing to the termination of their parental rights, they must understand that they're giving up all rights to the child forever. In the eyes of the law, they're no longer the parents.

Family lawyer Carl Devine says that typically if the grandparents are willing to adopt, the parent who is their child will agree. "It just makes it easier that way," Devine says. But he adds, "The other parent is not that easy an issue. The other parent must be served with legal papers. That other parent must be made aware of the adoption proceedings. And if the other parent does not agree to the termination, then it will have to go to court and proof be given as to why the person is not fit to be a parent."

An earlier chapter lists "extraordinary circumstances" that must be proved to have the court terminate parental rights against the will of one or both parents.[2]

When action of that sort is taken, it ruptures the family bond. It could mean that the grandparents will never see the child's parent— their son or daughter—again. It may create permanent hostility.

Hostility or rupture of the family bond is possible but not always inevitable. Sometimes adoptive grandparents and the biological parents can work out agreements so that the grandchildren and their birth parents can have some sort of comfortable relationship.

There are also reasons why grandparents may not or cannot adopt:

• It may not be financially advantageous to adopt.

If the child is removed from the parents because of abuse, neglect, abandonment, or any other reason, the state first looks for relatives who will take the child. In some states, even blood-kin grandparents or other relatives may be able to raise the grandchild as a foster parent. In that case, the grandparents are paid by the state just as any foster parent who is unrelated by blood to the child would be paid. These arrangements are usually called "kinship care." The downside is that the state retains legal custody of the child. The state will make decisions for the child. There's always a chance that the state would remove the child from your care. If grandparents or other relatives are willing to care for the child under this kind of custody arrangement, such a kinship placement is the state's first preference. If no relatives are available, then the child will be placed in foster care with people who may be strangers to the child.[3]

Relatives who take a child in kinship care sometimes complain that unrelated foster parents are paid more than they are for doing the same work. In some states this is true. The reasoning of state legislators in making such laws appears to be that if a person is blood kin to a child, there's some obligation to care for someone who is related, whereas foster parents are simply hired to do a job.

Recent federal legislation addresses, among other things, unequal pay for kinship care. The Fostering Connections to Succes and Increasing Adoptions Act is aimed at assisting grandparents and other relatives raising children whose parents cannot care for them. One part of the law is the Subsidized Guardianship Program, aimed at helping equalize pay to foster parents and relative caregivers. Another part of this legislation is to link caregivers to resources by providing accurate information about the benefits and services available to them.

An example of the benefits of this legislation is called the Kinship Guardianship Assistance Program (KinGAP). It gives states the option of using federal funds to help provide subsidized guardianship payments to relative caregivers for the support of children they are raising in foster care. As of this writing, thirty-nine states and the District of Columbia have subsidized guardianship programs.

As a condition for receiving federal foster care funding, state child welfare agencies are required to provide notice to all adult grandparents and other relatives that the state has removed a child from his or her parents' home. Such notice must be given within sixty days of the removal. The notice must explain the options available to the relatives. This allows grandparents and other relatives to decide early on if and to what extent they want to become involved with raising their grandchildren.[4]

State laws on kinship care vary. In different states it is called different things, and the legal options may be different from state to state. A family law attorney can help you decide what course of action is best in the state where you reside.

THE PROS AND CONS OF ADOPTING GRANDCHILDREN – 37

- In some states, a child in the home of grandparents or other relatives is eligible for state-paid medical care.

If you adopt the child, you'll lose state-paid medical care. Sometimes a child who is cared for by grandparents or is in foster care has health insurance coverage that is paid for by the state. If the child is adopted, this coverage ceases, since the state is no longer responsible for the child. The new adoptive parents are responsible for health insurance for the child, just as if the child had been born to them naturally.

- When a child is adopted, the adoptive parents assume liability responsibility for the child.

When the state places a child with relatives or non-relative foster parents under a custody arrangement, the state retains responsibility of making decisions for the child, and the grandparent or foster parent is a paid caregiver. If the child becomes aggressive, is a danger to others in the home, or commits a crime, the state is responsible. The child remains a ward of the state, not of the custodial caregiver.

- The court may ask an older child eligible for adoption with whom the child wants to live.

If the child wants to maintain a relationship with the natural parents—no matter how bad the parents are—the court may declare the child ineligible for adoption for this reason.

- Some grandparents don't want to adopt the child in hopes that the child's biological parents will someday be able to resume parenting their child.

Sometimes grandparents want their child to take back custody of the child at some future point and don't want to interfere with that relationship being put back together. As pointed out earlier, this hope is often unrealistic, and nothing is likely to change anytime soon. In the meantime, the child needs emotional and physical stability.

Waiting may be dangerous also because if the grandparent does not commit to the child's care, that grandparent runs the risk of losing the child altogether. As previously discussed, the state has probably given the biological parents a definite time limit in which to prove they are capable of parenting the child. If they don't get off drugs, get jobs, find a permanent place to live—whatever the requirements—within that time limit, the state will give the child to whoever has him or her at the time the state's waiting period ends. This doesn't necessarily mean you should move to adopt. Legal custody rather than adoption may be the best option in many cases. The point is to avoid waiting to put into place some sort of formal, court-directed custody arrangement or adoption relationship. Otherwise, there's a possibility that the child will be placed with someone else.

- Some grandparents believe the child's biological parents should be held accountable and responsible for the child.

Doris says that she and her husband, George, have not adopted their grandson, Travis, because they believe their son, Allen, the boy's father, should be responsible. Travis has lived with Doris and George all his life, and they have permanent custody. Travis is now eleven years old. Allen pays his parents child support regularly. "It isn't a lot of money," says Doris, "but we feel he should be forced to take some responsibility for his child." Allen was never married to Travis' mother, who is now out of the picture.

- Adoption is expensive. It can be frustrating and can take a long time.
- Adoption ends the right of the child to inherit from the birth parents. Adoption also makes the child ineligible to collect any public benefits for which the birth parents may be eligible.

Adoption does not mean the biological parents can't make gifts to the child or give the child an inheritance in their wills.

The bottom line is that once the child is released for adoption—involuntarily or voluntarily—and adoption is granted, the adoptive grandparents become the child's parents.

Some states have what is called *open adoption*. This is an adoption arrangement in which contact between the adoptive and biological parents is allowed or maintained. The exact arrangement and the level of openness varies widely from sending the biological mother report cards and photographs to having regularly scheduled visits for the child with the biological parents.

In *closed adoptions* there is no contact between the biological parents and the child and his or her adoptive parents. Usually medical and historical information about the child's heritage is made available to the adoptive parents. But in a closed adoption, the biological parents no longer have any right to see the child. This does not mean that *side agreements* can't be worked out. The adoptive parents may allow one or both of the biological parents to receive status reports on the child, including photographs and report cards. But the amount of contact is up to the adoptive parents.

Those favoring open adoption say this arrangement is better for the child. All children, they say, are entitled to information about their history and heritage. Those opposing it say the openness at best is temporary, with adoptive parents shutting off contact quickly. Opponents say open adoption may lead to charges later by the birth parent that he or she was promised or tricked into believing that there would be contact and that the promise was not honored. It is better, they say, to shut off contact, except as the adoptive parents may wish to grant it through side agreements.

Adoption of a child, whether a grandchild or not, is a life-changing decision. In increasing numbers courageous grandparents are willingly taking on a burden they were never intended to carry. Blessings on them.

The Lord gives wisdom generously to those who ask.

Lord, guide me as I make life-changing decisions.

Questions for Support Group Discussion

1. If any of your group adopted their grandchild or plan to adopt their grandchild, talk about what led them to make that decision.

2. If any of your group decided against adoption, talk about what led them to that decision.

4. Discuss the pros and cons of open adoption and closed adoption.

6. How has the termination of parental rights affected (or how do you expect it to affect) family relationships?

four

ATTACHMENT PROBLEMS

"I know what you want perfectly well, but I can't give it you, Dick. It isn't my fault; indeed it isn't. If I felt that I could care for anyone. . . But I don't feel that . . . I simply don't understand what the feeling means. . . . I despise myself quite enough as it is."

With these bitter words, Maisie, the young woman in Rudyard Kipling's novel *The Light that Failed*, turns down the offer of marriage from Dick, the man who loves her with all his heart. Dick wants to hold her close and kiss away the hurt. But she won't let him, even as she longs for a way out of her pain. Kipling's book was published in 1890.

These days we call Maisie's problem Reactive Attachment Disorder. As the great English novelist tells the story, Maisie grew up in what we now call foster care—the home of a stranger paid to raise the orphan child. The words he puts in Maisie's mouth are spot-on for the attitudes of the adult who was "unattached" as a child.

What is Reactive Attachment Disorder (RAD), and why is it important that grandparents who are raising their children's children understand it? While true RAD is rather rare, and attachment problems are not inevitable, many children being raised by grandparents have been abused, neglected, shuffled among caregivers, perhaps even malnourished, to the point that it's almost expected that grandparents raising grandchildren will encounter special parenting problems, including attachment disorders. The time-honored parenting methods they used on their first set of children may not work with these kids.

Grandparents are not the only ones who may encounter unattached children. Adoptive parents of children who were several years old when they were taken away from neglectful parents or came out of the foster care system to an adoptive home may contend with the same deep emotional scarring. Like Maisie, these children cannot give love because they don't know what it is. They have no model for mutual self-giving.

If there's one thing such children have learned in their short lives, it's that adults are not trustworthy. Adults don't meet your needs. Frightened and distrustful of everyone, such a child may be too young to reason it out in words, but his or her reaction is to push adults away. At the same time, he or she makes every effort to stay in control of his or her own destiny, since, as the child sees it, no adult is going to help. He or she is trying to call all the shots, and when grown, the unattached child, like Maisie, may be unable to form any lasting relationships.

The terms "attachment" and "bonding" are sometimes used interchangeably. They aren't quite the same. "Bonding" refers to the involuntary development of emotional bond that occurs without conscious thought or effort. Bonding occurs very early and automatically in normal parent-child situations.[1]

By contrast, attachment is a learned behavior. "Attachment" describes the normal emotional connection that infants and children develop toward their parents or other regular caregivers. Because people are different, attachment problems form a continuum, ranging from little or no attachment problems in some children to full-blown RAD so severe the persons have difficulty developing emotional attachments to anyone. Intensive therapeutic parenting to correct early damage may be necessary.[2]

All these circumstances create special parenting problems for grandparents, adoptive parents, or other caregivers who come into the child's life when he or she is several years old. After being in foster care, perhaps with several families, or after he or she has been removed from neglectful or abusive parents, these problems may present themselves.

Remember Jacob, the four-year-old we met earlier whose biological parents dropped him off with his grandmother, Alice, at 3:00 A.M. one Saturday?

When Jacob first landed on her doorstep, Alice sensed that the child needed stability and order. Over the next weeks, she was careful to establish a routine. If she went out, she took Jacob with her. She did not leave him with sitters. They always came back to the same house. He slept in a real bed, the same one every night. Alice could tell Jacob thought it was strange, even a little uncomfortable. It wasn't like sleeping on the floor of the car in a different parking lot each night.

She fed him three times a day at approximately the same times. Alice tried to explain who she was. She told him to call her "Grandma," so he did, but it was clear that the word carried no special meaning for him. It was just one more name in a long line of strangers. Family and generations were new ideas, too much for a four-year-old to grasp.

Four years later, when Jacob was eight, Grandma was hanging in there, holding the fort for Jacob. Gradually Jacob began to trust Alice when he saw that she was always there. She didn't get high and forget to fix him something to eat. Still, in Jacob's experience you can't count on adults. Some day Grandma might leave as quickly as she came. It's safer to stay in control yourself.

As time went on, Jacob gained weight. He grew taller. His grandmother thought he was beginning to relax. But Jacob's "mean streak," as Alice calls it, persists. She does not understand why parenting Jacob is so different from raising his father, Lewis.

Like the rainy afternoon when Jacob got off the school bus at the end of the unpaved driveway.

His grandmother, Alice, met him at the door. "Please take off those wet, muddy shoes before you come in," she said.

"Make me," said the eight-year-old, darting past her.

Why does he do things like that? Alice wondered, surveying the trail of mud on the carpet. Alice knows that every child is sometimes disobedient. But with Jacob these things happened all the time.

She wonders why he seems to enjoy annoying her. She wonders if there's a connection with the comments Miss Williams, his third-grade teacher, writes at the bottom of his report card. "Jacob does not relate well to other children," the message says. Or sometimes it says, "Jacob is touchy and blames others for his mistakes."

With all his troubles, Jacob does fairly well in school, though now and then the school sends a note home saying he's been fighting again. Alice has watched him stir up trouble between other children. He seemed to enjoy watching the ensuing battle. His father was never like that when he was little. Alice wonders why Jacob is different. How is she supposed to parent such a child?

In the four years Jacob has lived with her, Alice has done her best to be consistent in her discipline. She loves Jacob and tells him so. She tries to model a loving attitude always. On Sundays they go to Sunday School and church. Yet Jacob is defiant and often angry for no reason Alice can figure out. *What am I doing wrong?* Alice asks herself. *I gummed up raising his father; otherwise, he'd be raising Jacob instead of doing jail time for dealing drugs. Now I've messed up again. I must be a terrible parent.*

Alice may have made mistakes in raising Lewis, Jacob's father. What parent doesn't? But she should not blame herself for some of the things she sees in Jacob. He existed in the confusion of drug-abusing, alcohol-soaked parents for the first four years of his life. His father was in and out of jail. His mother was often high or drinking. She parked her son with her parents, her friends, people he had never seen before. He was in and out of various day cares, so he never formed a bond with anyone who stuck around. Once a babysitter locked him in a room with two big dogs and went out. He was three years old.

When Jacob was coming to consciousness in the first years of his life, he had no anchors, no harbors, no lighthouses that didn't move. This woman who calls herself "Grandma" is just one more stranger in a long line. Why should Jacob trust her or any other adult? Adults were never there for him when he needed them. He is unattached.[3]

Normal mother-child attachment forms during the first two years of life. Otto Kaak, University of Kentucky psychiatrist and an authority on attachment issues, says that six months to two years of age is the prime time for learning social attachment.[4] With the same caregiver and consistent expectations, attachment develops. If the child uses the same route in his or her brain often enough, it becomes a kind of mental and emotional interstate highway. The child has attached. The child knows this person and trusts this person because this person meets his or her needs.

Attachment is crucial to the child's emotional, mental, and physical development. If, however, the child has been bounced from one relative to another or moved through several foster-care homes or a series of caregivers, attachment problems may confront grandparents, adoptive parents, and other caregivers when they come on the scene months or years into a child's life. In fact, children adopted after the age of six months are at risk for attachment problems. "Every move from one placement to another is *trauma* for the child."[5]

The ability to trust and to develop satisfactory inter-personal relationships grows from successful attachment. If the bonding-attachment process is disrupted early in a child's life, perhaps when he or she is between two and three years old, either because of the abuse and neglect of parents or because of ever-changing, inconsistent caregivers, the child may learn to fear any close emotional relationship. The child may also believe that the reason adults treat him or her badly is because he or she is unlovable. *If I were better, they would quit going away and leaving me,* the unattached child reasons. Since he or she can't please or trust anybody, why try at all?[6]

When dealing with children rescued from abuse and neglect, it's hard to know whether what you are seeing is normal childhood difficulties or deficits growing from neglect in infancy and early childhood. If it's the latter, without therapeutic intervention, the effects may persist into adulthood with disastrous results on the person's ability to succeed in school and work. This is why grandparents struggling to parent a child who has experienced neglect in early life should be aware that such a thing as RAD exists, even though full-blown attachment disorder is rather rare.

In a normal parent-child relationship, as the infant comes to consciousness, the child feels loved. His or her own self-esteem develops. He or she must be somebody worth loving, or this adult wouldn't take care of him or her. The child gradually realizes that when this person who loves him or her says no, the caregiver does it with the child's good in mind. The child is influenced by the parent and attaches to the parent at a deep, emotional level that will make a lifelong difference to the child. If the child feels warmth and love and approval from the parent or other primary caregiver, preferably almost always the same person, then if the caregiver does not approve of something the child does and corrects him or her, the child will pay attention to the instruction and discipline.[7]

Another expression of lack of attachment may be manipulation by the child. The youngster believes he or she can't count on anybody, that no one person is ever there for very long, and that nobody cares about him or her and his or her needs. The child concludes that maneuvering for control is the way to get things. The child becomes overly friendly, never meeting a stranger. The child may "make nice" to get his or her own way—then, in an expression of inner rage at the uncertainties of life, may cut off the cat's tail or torture the dog. Children with severe cases of RAD should not be allowed to have pets until their hearts have been healed of the anger.[8]

Reactive attachment disorder begins before age five and appears to grow from extreme neglect in the first three years of life. There are three signs of RAD:

- The child is unable to form attachments, forming relationships only when he or she has a need. One caregiver is as good as another; the child doesn't care, just as long as he or she gets what he or she wants.

- RAD children typically have trouble with cause-and-effect thinking. Development is retarded in the area of understanding concepts. The grandparent may say, "You must do your homework or stay in your room for thirty minutes—take a time-out." The unattached child thinks a time-out isn't such a bad idea, since he or she is accustomed to being beaten and starved. The child sees doing homework versus time alone in his or her room as a choice, not a punishment. When the child does not do homework, in the child's mind he or she has simply chosen the other consequence offered—a time-out. Then the child is puzzled because the grandparent is upset. Alice finds that Jacob does not understand punishment because he does not connect it with what he did.[9]

- RAD children may be impulsive, aggressive, and totally lacking in remorse. They do not want to be parented. These children want to be—need to be—in control, as Jacob was when he ran across the carpet with muddy shoes. Symptoms may include chronic lying and low self-esteem. RAD children tend to form superficial relationships and display affection for everyone they meet. The outsider thinks, *My, what a friendly child!* The child thinks, *What can I take this sucker for?*[10]

A condition called "disinhibited RAD" can also occur. The child may say things that indicate attachment, but it's superficial, as when the overly friendly child does not have a small child's normal fear of new persons. He or she will go with any stranger who asks him or her. If you suspect this form of RAD, observe the child carefully. Be certain cuddles and a child looking attached is real attachment and not a superficial act to manipulate you. In fact, others may wonder why you complain of parenting problems since the child is always so sweet in public.[11]

Another source of potential bonding or attachment problems may be that caregivers are putting children in the care of others outside the home at earlier and earlier ages. The increase in state-funded preschool programs has brought a shift in thinking and a steady rise in the number of children in preschool. More than one million children were enrolled in public preschool programs in 2005, up 63 percent from 1995.[12] Parents' long workdays may result in very young children spending more waking hours in daycare than they spend with their parents. Childcare facilities, like nursing homes, are notorious for rapid turnover in employees. While these persons may be well intentioned, the resulting revolving-door caregivers, plus the long hours, may leave young children with little sense of permanence or stability.

Since attachment is a process,[13] if at all possible, a month or six weeks of transition time, some of it supervised by a professional, is best when a child must be transferred from one caregiver to another. This may occur when a child several years old is being moved to a new living environment. The new adoptive parents, or grandparents assuming custody, may visit the child in his or her present home. Then the current caregivers may bring the child to visit in the new home. At other times they may all meet together at a neutral place. Because in our culture so many children are being moved from natural parents to foster parents to adoptive parents, or some combination of shifting the child from place to place, some cities have buildings known as professional third-party contractor facilities maintained specifically to help with these transitions. Visits continue until the child is comfortable, with attachment gradually shifting to the adoptive parents or other new caregivers.

Adoptive parents should guard against treating the child like a guest on these visits. He or she should be a member of the family from the outset.[14] Five-year-old David met his about-to-be adoptive parents at a Holiday Inn on several occasions during transition visits. When he finally went with his adoptive family to their middle-class, three-bedroom ranch house, he felt deceived. "Where's the big house?" he asked. The five-year-old thought the Holiday Inn with its spacious foyer and big swimming pool was where his new family lived.

Transition time is not always possible. Sometimes a government agency must remove a child swiftly, even forcibly, from parents or other caregivers when there are urgent abuse, neglect, and safety issues. This sets the child up for attachment/bonding problems. Without transition time, parked with one more stranger, it's not difficult to see why that child may wind up unattached, feeling worthless, that nobody cares, and that all adults are untrustworthy.

Attention Deficit Hyperactive Disorder (ADHD) and Oppositional Defiant Disorder (ODD) may be the result of attachment problems. They are more fully discussed in a future chapter.

Just as the damage done with lack of early bonding and attachment is a process, so is the cure. The child tests it. Over time, he or she can relax and decide that you do mean it when you say you love him or her. You are there for the child when he or she needs you.

What matters is relationship. Dr. Kaak, the University of Kentucky psychiatrist, says that the grandparent or other caregiver may think, *I'm sick of this child's manipulations.* Of course, you are! But think therapeutically. Try to understand the reasons why the child thinks he or she needs to control you. Remember that what the child has been told by others, as well as by you, helps form an "inner working model" of what the child thinks of himself or herself—*I'm just a foster child, I'll never amount to anything; nobody wants me; I'll move again soon, I won't live here long.*[15]

In Jacob's case, at the age of four, after instinctive attempts to bond to his natural parents had been thwarted by their inconsistent parenting of him, followed by what he understood as his parents' desertion of him, he saw no reason to trust anyone. Repeatedly the little boy had no transition time or opportunity to adjust emotionally or physically to new surroundings and people. This break in the early attachment relationship is a probable cause of some of his grandmother's parenting problems.

How should grandparents and other responsible persons parent children who appear to have some degree of attachment disorder?

One important key to successful reattachment is for the parent to be in control.[16] What Jacob's grandmother, Alice, did instinctively—establish a routine—is a good start. If a child's parents are abusing drugs, he or she probably has known only a disorganized home environment. One of the best things you can do for such a child—or any young child—is establish a routine. It is crucial in managing a child with ADHD or ODD.

Nancy Thomas, therapeutic parenting specialist, and her husband, Jerry, have shared their home with severely emotionally disturbed children for more than twenty years. Thomas says five things are necessary to help the unattached child. She notes that such a child does not want affection because his or her experience with it has been painful. He or she wants to avoid close relationships. However, the disturbed child must not be allowed to be in control; you must be in control.

The tools are the following:

Eye contact. It must be soft and loving. Look into the child's eyes lovingly whether he or she is acting pleasant and cute or angry and defiant. The child will try to avoid it. But with compassion and firmness, make the child accept your loving eye contact.

Touch. We need twelve hugs a day for emotional healing, Thomas says. But the disturbed child is not allowed to ask for hugs. Do not let him or her reverse roles. You, the parent, not the child, control loving interaction. A loving parent gives plenty of hugs. The disturbed child learns to trust that the parent will do so. Hugs should come at random times.

Movement stimulates our brains. Rocking the child, dancing around with the child in your arms, letting him or her use a small trampoline or ride a horse—all are therapeutic.

Smiles. Bounce a smile into your child's eyes several times a day. If he or she returns it, the child is in good shape. If not, the child may need therapeutic help.

Sugar. Human milk is the sweetest of all milks. Thomas recommends combining warm milk with sugar as a treat that reinforces the bonding process.

Snuggle time. Set aside a special time for holding the child in your arms in a comfortable rocking chair. Snuggle time is fun time, with nursery rhymes or songs and stories.

Thomas emphasizes that the disturbed child is not in charge of hugs and snuggle time. "These bonding techniques are like heart medication for a child's broken heart," she says. Thomas adds that you wouldn't let a child choose a medication and determine the dosage, so don't allow it with these emotional medicines. You—the healthy adult—give hugs and snuggles, not because the child is lovable at that moment. Don't show affection on a schedule, she warns. Give it often and with little warning.[17]

**God will give you the strength to
be up to the challenges you face.**

Lord, teach me the best way to parent this hurting child.

Questions for Support Group Discussion

1. Discuss events in your grandchild's life that you believe may create problems as you parent the child.

2. Does anyone in the group suspect attachment problems in his or her grandchild? If so, talk about the effects these are having in the home.

3. Discuss the symptoms of RAD and ways to help a child who is experiencing it.

4. If group members are feeling manipulated by their grandchildren, discuss specific instances of manipulation they have experienced and ways to deal with it effectively.

five

ATTENTION-DEFICIT/ HYPERACTIVITY DISORDER (ADHD) AND OPPOSITIONAL DEFIANT DISORDER (ODD)

"I called to Bobby, but he wouldn't come—every time I started toward him, he darted in another direction," Phyllis said. "I chased him up and down the mall until I was out of breath and people were staring at us. He was like a wild little animal that had escaped its cage. The security guard tried to catch him, but the kid zoomed into the street. Somehow all the cars missed him. Finally he collided with someone coming out of the drug store, and it slowed him down enough that I could grab him. I apologized to the person he ran into. The man was pleasant, but I could tell he wondered why I didn't have the child under control."

Phyllis is fifty years old and divorced. Bobby, five years old, is the oldest of the four children by four fathers whom Phyllis's daughter, Connie, gave birth to. Phyllis is raising Bobby. The second baby was given up for adoption. The third and fourth babies both died at birth, not unusual for children born to a heavily drug- and alcohol-addicted mother. Connie remains addicted. Between hitches in jail she lives on the streets of Sacramento, her hometown. From time to time she lives with the most recent new boyfriend. "She hasn't hit bottom yet," Phyllis says.

"My daughter and her boyfriend beat Bobby one night a couple of years ago," Phyllis explains. After that incident local authorities removed Bobby from his mother's care and called Phyllis to ask if she and her husband would take him. They agreed. The next year Phyllis's twenty-five-year marriage unraveled. Bobby spends some time with his grandfather, who also lives in Sacramento, but mostly he lives with Phyllis, who gave up her career in public relations to raise him.

Phyllis' experience with Bobby—what she calls his *wild animal act*—is an all-too-common occurrence encountered by grandparents and others who are raising children rescued from abuse and neglect. These grandparents find themselves with parenting problems unlike any they endured with the children they raised years earlier. "It's hard to know whether I'm seeing normal childhood rambunctiousness," says Phyllis, "or behavioral problems that will persist into adulthood with disastrous results on Bobby's ability to succeed in school and work."

While not inevitable, many grandparents raising grandchildren find themselves dealing with the special needs of a child caused by early abuse or neglect.

One of the more common conditions creating problems for the new parents of children who have been abused or neglected in infancy and early childhood or who have had inconsistent care because of multiple caregivers is attention-deficit/hyperactivity disorder (ADHD). Although it may be one result of attachment problems, children who have not been abused or neglected sometimes have ADHD as well. A closely allied behavior problem frequently accompanying ADHD is oppositional defiant disorder (ODD). In this chapter we will center on the parenting problems created by ADHD and ODD.

While not usually diagnosed until a child starts school, Bobby's pediatrician recently told Phyllis that he thinks Bobby has ADHD. He's having trouble paying attention in kindergarten. Phyllis wonders what will happen next year when he starts first grade. "Why is he like that?" she asks. "He acts as if he's wound up on a spring and can't stop."

Is ADHD for real, or is it simply an expression of normal childhood energy? Any child can be difficult sometimes because young children are naturally very active. All healthy children display wiggly, squirmy hyperactivity from time to time. Short attentions spans are common in small children. In older children or teenagers, their attention span often depends upon how interested they are in the task at hand.

"That boy needs a boss—that's all," says Fred, Phyllis's ex-husband and Bobby's grandfather. "Paddle his bottom and tell him to sit down and hush."

Is Fred right? Is a firm hand all Bobby needs? What is ADHD anyway?

ADHD is a common behavior problem in children, affecting from four to twelve percent of school-aged children. About three times more boys than girls are diagnosed with ADHD.[1] Some experts believe more boys than girls are diagnosed because girls' symptoms of ADHD are different than boys'. Boys with ADHD tend to be hyperactive, doing things to gain attention, while girls with ADHD are more often inattentive daydreamers.[2] How can a child with ADHD be distinguished from one displaying normal childhood behavior? Symptoms of ADHD include two groups of behavior symptoms:

- Inattention
- Hyperactivity-impulsive behavior.

Not all children will have all the symptoms. Generally children must show six or more signs or symptoms from each category for at least six months to be diagnosed with ADHD. Before a diagnosis of ADHD is made, the symptoms are determined to affect the child's ability to function both at home and at school. If the problem is with just one teacher or with only the parents, then perhaps something else is going on. Another determination to be made in diagnosing ADHD is whether the child's friendships with other children are affected.[3]

Warning signs of *inattention* include

• Trouble sustaining attention during work or play.

• Inability to listen to directions even when spoken to directly.

• Difficulty following through on instructions and failure to finish tasks.

• Disorganization.

• Avoidance or resistance to tasks that require sustained mental effort.

• Ease of distraction.

• Forgetfulness or a habit of continually losing important items.

Warning signs of *hyperactivity-impulsive behavior* include

• Fidgeting and squirming frequently.

• Running, jumping, or climbing when inappropriate. An older child may be constantly restless.

• Inability to play quietly—always on the go.

• Speaking without thinking, talking excessively.

• Frequent trouble taking turns.

• Calling out answers before the question is completed.

• Interrupting others' conversations or games.

ADHD seems to run in families. About one in four children with ADHD has a relative with the disorder.[4]

Inherited tendency does not explain all cases of ADHD, nor do abuse and neglect. Children born to mothers who used tobacco and alcohol while pregnant are at greater risk of ADHD than others. Other risk factors for ADHD include premature delivery, significantly low birth weight, and high body lead levels. A head injury during childhood can also contribute to the development of ADHD.[5]

Infant malnutrition, always a peril when parents neglect a child, is a strong risk indicator of ADHD. Even if the child gets enough food later on, infants who suffer from malnutrition may develop behavior problems. The most common is ADHD.[6]

Child psychologist James Dobson, founder of Focus on the Family, reports that forty percent of three-month-old infants are exposed to television regularly. "The likelihood of hyperactive disorders [like ADHD] later in life grows by 10 percent with each hour of daily TV viewing before age 3," according to a Focus publication.[7]

ADHD is the most common mental health issue for children and adolescents who have been diagnosed with fetal alcohol syndrome (FAS). Caused by the birth mother's consumption of alcohol at conception or while pregnant, this devastating birth defect is now the leading known environmental cause of physical birth defects.[8] Pregnant women should not drink alcohol at all. No safe level of alcohol consumption is known. Alcohol and drug abuse during pregnancy may reduce production of neurotransmitters in the developing brain of the unborn child. Neurotransmitters are chemical messengers that enable parts of the brain to communicate with each other. Abnormal brain chemicals may contribute to ADHD, affecting both mental and emotional functioning.[9]

The amount of alcohol and the timing of its use influence the amount of damage done to the child. The earlier in the pregnancy, the worse the damage is likely to be. Alcohol is especially dangerous during the first trimester.

Although Bobby has not yet been diagnosed with FAS, it is likely that his problems began before he was born because of his mother's excessive use of alcohol.

Fetal alcohol syndrome is diagnosed by three criteria:

- Growth problems: children with FAS may be smaller in height and/or weight compared with other children their age.
- Facial abnormalities. Children with FAS tend to have thin upper lips, no philtrum (the groove that runs from the base of the nose to the upper lip), small eyes, and a small head.

- Hyperactivity, learning and behavioral problems, and short attention span.[10]

The use of cocaine or crack cocaine by the mother during pregnancy can cause premature birth and frailty as well as the infant's addiction at birth to the mother's drug of choice. Although early symptoms may disappear, long-term effects may include learning, behavioral, or medical difficulties.

Even legal prescriptions or over-the-counter drugs can create problems for the unborn.

Another common condition found in children whose early lives have been difficult is oppositional defiant disorder (ODD). Less common than ADHD, oppositional defiant disorder produces similar symptoms. Children with ODD are hostile and disobedient toward parents, caregivers, or other authority figures. Behaviors may include, among others,

- Frequent temper tantrums.
- Argumentativeness with adults.
- Refusal to comply with adult requests or rules.
- Deliberate annoyance of other people.
- Blaming others for their mistakes and bad behavior.
- Ease of being annoyed.
- Anger and resentment.
- Spiteful or vindictive behavior.
- Aggressiveness toward peers.
- Avoidance of eye contact.
- Destructiveness to self, others, and material things.
- Lack of conscience.

Oppositional defiant disorder is a complex problem, and no clear cause is known. A genetic component—that is, the child's natural temperament—coupled with some or all of the following factors increase the risk of ODD:

- A parent who abuses substances.
- A parent who had ADHD or ODD.

- Abuse or neglect.
- Lack of supervision, a frequent problem with children of alcohol and drug-addicted parents.
- Family instability, multiple moves, frequent changes in schools or daycare providers.[11]

No cure exists for ADHD or ODD, but there are things that can be done if your grandchild struggles with it. Here are some suggestions:

- Evidence is increasing that there is a biological basis or that early childhood experiences contribute to ADHD. Do not feel guilty or blame yourself.
- Establish a routine for getting up, going to bed, eating, and being on time for school or appointments.
- Set firm boundaries with consistent consequences for violations.
- Try to spend more time with the child. Dinner together at a regular time is a good place to start.
- Plan ahead what your response to infractions of rules will be so that you can be calm and unemotional when the child's opposition erupts.
- Praise the child's good behaviors.
- Give the child a bit of control by offering acceptable choices.
- Seek professional help.

Become the child's best advocate. That can be done in several ways.

First, become an expert on both ADHD and its frequent accompanying ailment, ODD. They both occur for some of the same reasons.

Keep a record of all information concerning the child, including doctor or therapist evaluations and records of the child's prior treatments if any.

At the beginning of the school year, ask for a meeting with the child's teacher, the principal, or someone designated by the principal to represent him or her, and the special education teacher if the school has one. Take an active role in forming a team to help the child.

Know the child's rights under the Individuals with Disabilities Education Act (IDEA) and Section 504 of the Rehabilitation Act. Visit <www.taalliance.org> to find the information center in your state where you can learn more about these pieces of legislation.[12]

Help the child learn from his or her mistakes. Persons with ADHD sometimes have difficulty making the connection between their behavior and the consequences. Explain why what he or she did—or did not do—is unacceptable and upsetting to you. Be firm but unemotional. Don't yell.

Find a support group or parenting class to help you learn more techniques to improve your management of a small child with special problems or your relationship with an older one.

As previously pointed out, one of the most crucial things you can do for a child with ADHD or ODD—or any young child— is to establish regular habits. If a child's parents were abusing drugs before he or she came to live with the grandparents, he or she probably knew only a chaotic home environment. The same things that helped Jacob, the four-year-old we talked about in the first chapter, helped Bobby, the little boy we met at the beginning of this chapter. Those things were routine, familiarity with the surroundings, and habits. Bobby, like Jacob, learned stability by knowing that when he and his grandmother went out, they always came back to the same house. He slept in the same room in the same bed every night. Bobby's grandmother, Phyllis, established a bedtime routine. She attempts to have two meals a day—three on weekends—served regularly and at approximately the same time. Bobby did not adjust overnight, but in the time he has lived with his grandmother, he has become a far different and much-improved child from the angry, frightened urchin the social worker delivered to his grandparents two years ago.

Sometimes doctors or psychologists suggest medicine for children with ADHD or ODD. Ritalin is probably the best known of the numerous prescription drugs on the market for children with ADHD. These are usually stimulant medications thought to restore balance to brain chemicals associated with the parts of the brain that control attention and movement. If medication is being considered for the child or children for whom you are responsible, check frequently with the child's physician. Like all drugs, medicine intended to help ADHD can have side effects or unpleasant, even dangerous, reactions. You and your doctor must decide which of the many ADHD drugs, if any, is right for your child. The hope is that the drug will enable the child to focus better on his or her schoolwork and other tasks. Although experts assure us that taking one of the drugs used to treat ADHD will not turn a child into a zombie or alter the child's personality, a grandparent's hesitation to give the drug is understandable, especially if one or both of his or her parents is an addict.

ADHD affects all of a child's relationships—friends, family, teachers, and others. The symptoms of ADHD may change, but it doesn't usually just go away by itself. Each case is individual, and drug therapy is not right for everyone. You and the child's doctor may decide drugs are not right for this particular child. The doctor may also suggest professional behavior therapy or counseling.[13]

Consider writing a home rules contract (HRC) if you are dealing with an older child or a teenager. The primary purpose of an HRC is a way to hold the teen accountable for his or her behavior. Pick a relaxed time and sit down with the child and work on it together. Decide ahead of time what rules you want to include in the contract—but not more than five. Too many can be confusing. These should be problem areas that as a parent or parent figure you believe need improvement and for which the child or teen should be held accountable.

These may or may not include such things as curfew, alcohol and drug use, chores, school behavior and grades, smoking, telephone and computer use, running away, compliance with the medication schedule if the young person is on a regular medicine, such as Ritalin. Any area that is difficult for you and the teen you are raising can be included.

Be sure the child is given an opportunity for his or her input. Ask for the child's suggestions on how to manage or reach a compromise on contentious situations. The contract will set forth basic rules, consequences and privileges, and a set of expectations that adults have for the teen or preteen. It is important that all teens and preteens in the household are included in the HRC. The contract should not be used to single out one child for bad behavior. To be considered fair, everyone must be included. Give everyone who will be subject to the contract an opportunity to have input, including suggestions as to what the consequences for violations should be. List the privileges that can be earned by living up to the terms of the contract.

Other adults in the home who are not actively involved in the process of raising the teen should be excluded from the contract. It is between the teen or preteen and his principal caregivers, whether that is the natural parents, adoptive parents, or a grandparent. Do not complicate the issue by attempting to let other adults, for example, an aunt or uncle who lives with the family, add other ideas to the mix. If these individuals have a problem with the child, they should tell you, the chief caregiver, and let you handle it.

Sometimes it may be necessary to have a social worker or a counselor sit in on the negotiations to act as mediator between caregivers and the child. When the teen does things right, be sure to praise him or her.[14]

If the inability to focus, prioritize, obey instructions, and finish school projects is significantly affecting a child's ability to function either at home or at school, it may be time to seek professional help. Psychiatrists, psychologists, pediatricians, or family physicians and neurologists can diagnose ADHD, and all of these can help you develop parenting skills for dealing with special needs children.

Perhaps what you are experiencing in the child is the normal hyperactivity of early childhood. If you are a grandparent who has suddenly taken up parenting again, you may have forgotten how high the energy level is in a young child. If the child is older, it may be the moodiness that sometimes besets teenagers that is causing difficulties.

On the other hand, you may have a problem. Either way, do not try to go it alone. If you have no money for a private physician, a call to your Department of Social Services (or whatever similar name it goes by in the area where you live) should put you in touch with medical help. This agency should also be able to recommend parenting classes and help you locate support groups in which you can share problems and learn new approaches for dealing with a child whose early life experiences have made him or her hard to parent. Asking for help is not admitting failure—it's acknowledgment that one person cannot know everything.

If you are struggling with a difficult situation and child, remember what Joan Callander says is one of her personal "aha" moments: "You don't have to be afraid of tomorrow, because God is already there."[15]

Our God is a God of peace, not confusion.

*God, help me establish good structure
and calm surroundings for my grandchild.*

Questions for Support Group Discussion

1. ADHD and ODD are both common today, especially in children who have had rough starts in life. What if any behaviors are the grandparents in your group experiencing that lead them to believe their grandchildren may have one of these disorders?

2. If any of the grandparents in your group feel their grandchild has fetal alcohol syndrome, discuss the signs and symptoms of FAS.

3. Discuss reasons that children removed from their birth parents often develop these or other emotional problems.

4. Discuss the value of a Home Rules Contract.

six

RECOGNIZING ABUSE

"When Allyn was eight years old, she suddenly went from being a happy-go-lucky, laid-back child to angry, sullen, and defiant," Sally said. "It was almost as if she were walking around with a chip on her shoulder all the time. She began to talk back and screamed at me over nothing. It was classic sexual abuse symptoms, but her father and I didn't recognize them at all. Besides, we never dreamed that the eighteen-year-old son of close friends would do such a thing.

"Allyn didn't say anything. Needless to say, the boy and his parents—our good friends—didn't mention it. When Allyn began her teenage years she began to purposely gain weight until she was quite heavy. We now realize she was trying to make herself unattractive to males.

"Finally, when she was twenty-one years old and in her third year of college, her anger was so intense that we insisted she see a therapist. One day she came home from a therapy session and screamed, 'I hate you!' and it came tumbling out. We learned that our good friends' son sodomized her, perhaps on two or three occasions. There may have been other episodes of sexual abuse. It happened when she was eight, but we did not hear about it until thirteen years later." Sally surmises that Allyn eventually told the whole story to a therapist, but she does not think that her daughter has yet shared with her all that happened.

An earlier chapter tells the circumstances of Allyn's pregnancy and her parents' decision to adopt Allyn's child, Cody, their grandchild. Allyn is the middle child of their three daughters. Ed and Sally were grateful that his law practice flourished, even though it meant long hours at the office and that Ed didn't always get to the girls' ball games and recitals. But, good daddy that he is, Ed made up for it by planning happy times with his girls on other occasions. As the girls got older, Sally became her husband's office manager.

During those thirteen long years of silence and misunderstanding, Sally and Ed could never figure out Allyn's abrupt personality shift. How do you parent a child who is filled with anger and self-hatred?

"When the girls began to look for colleges," Sally says, "I insisted that they pick out-of-state schools. I didn't want them trailing home every weekend. I felt they needed to develop their own identities and learn to make decisions."

"Did it work?" I asked.

"It worked beautifully with Donna and Jennifer, the oldest and the youngest. Donna went to Emory University in Atlanta, where she and her husband and their two children now live. She is elegant, sophisticated, all I could have hoped for in a daughter. The youngest, Jennifer, graduated from the University of Michigan at Ann Arbor. She's married to a lawyer and lives in Chicago. They have one child and another on the way.

"For Allyn, that plan was disastrous. It was a struggle to get her to college at all. She was so angry, and we had no idea why. She finally agreed to enter the University of Richmond, right here in town. She actually made pretty good grades and was just about a year short of graduation when Ed and I saw more changes in her behavior and realized she was using drugs. It was crack cocaine, highly addictive, and especially dangerous for women to use. During this time she met Charlie, a man about her age, in a bar. He was using drugs as well."

The year after Allyn finally was able to tell her mother at least something about the sexual abuse she had suffered thirteen years earlier, she became pregnant by her boyfriend, Charlie. She dropped out of college in her last year. In the end, Allyn's abuse and neglect of her child was so great that the state terminated Allyn's and Charlie's parental rights. Allyn's parents, Sally and Ed, adopted the little girl. Cody is now eleven years old.

This family's experience with child sexual abuse fits the description of a classic case. The victim knew her abuser. The victim became so angry it permanently distorted her life. No one learned of the abuse until years after the attacks. She gained weight to make herself unattractive. These events are typical in such cases.

As a grandparent, you would not have full parental responsibility for your grandchild unless some kind of severe rupture had occurred in the child's birth home. Not every child who ends up in the care of grandparents or another relative or caregiver has been abused, of course. But it is common enough that grandparents who are parenting again should know the physical and behavioral signs of child sexual abuse.

What behaviors should raise a question as to whether the child has been or is being abused? What can you do to prevent abuse of a child in your care?

Sexual abuse may be the most common form of mistreatment. As many as ninety percent of special needs children have been sexually abused in some way.[1] What is child sexual abuse? Why does it generate life-changing anger and other strong emotions in the victim? Why do victims, even after they are grown up, refuse to talk about it? What are the signs to watch for? How do you parent a child who has been abused?

Child abuse is "any behavior directed toward a child by a parent, guardian, care giver, other family member, or other adult, that endangers or impairs a child's physical or emotional health and development."[2]

Some state laws define four types of abuse.

1. Physical abuse is non-accidental injury of a child by a parent or other caregiver. Injuries may range from superficial bruises and welts to broken bones, burns, and serious internal injury. Sometimes death results from physical abuse.

2. Physical neglect is withholding or failing to provide adequate food, shelter, or other basic needs and/or supervision so that the child is at imminent risk of being impaired physically, mentally, or emotionally. Neglect may be more harmful to the child than some forms of active abuse.

Consider Tommy, for example. Tommy was born to a pair of drug and alcohol users who lived in their car on the streets of Omaha. He spent the first six months of his life sitting in a car seat. His drug-addicted parents changed his diaper now and then and fed him when they thought about it. They never held him, cuddled him, or talked to him. Nobody comforted him when he cried. Someone reported Tommy's plight to social services, and the authorities removed him from his parents and called his grandparents and said, "Please come pick up the child."

"That's how much notice we got that we had another child to raise," says Glenn, his grandfather, echoing the words of other grandparents whose stories are told in this book. Tommy's muscle development was retarded because he had never used his muscles. "He just sat in the car seat," his grandfather says. "His social development was almost like that of a newborn." The grandparents never found out who reported the neglect. They are just grateful it happened before more damage was done.

3. Sexual abuse is when a parent or caretaker commits a sexual offense against a child or allows a sexual offense to be committed. This can range from rape and sodomy to engaging the child in sexual or pornographic activity, including forcing the child to take part in such activity.[3]

The greatest risk of sexual abuse of a child comes from friends and family, not strangers. A child molester is usually someone known to the child, a trusted adult or older teen. This person could be a close friend or family member, a babysitter, neighbor, or coach. The molester may be a skilled manipulator who uses special attention, gifts, force, or guilt to further his or her purposes. He or she may use lies or threats of harm to the child's family to frighten the child into cooperation and silence.[4] "Half of all child molesters are under the age of thirty-one and only about ten percent are more than fifty years of age."[5] Parent Child Abuse New York says, "Ninety-three percent of victims know their abusers; thirty-four percent are abused by family members; fifty-nine percent are abused by someone trusted by the family."[6]

4. Emotional abuse includes parents' or caregivers' acts or omissions that cause or could cause "serious conduct, cognitive, affective, or other mental disorders. For example, torture, close confinement, or the constant use of verbally abusive language to harshly criticize and denigrate a child."[7] Close confinement may include such things as wrapping the child in sheets or blankets so tightly that he or she cannot move or even breathe well. Some of the now-discredited "rebirthing" techniques included close confinement. Cases of "rebirthing" have been recorded that ended in the child dying of suffocation.

Short attention spans and difficulty with concentrating are just the tip of the iceberg for the victims of varying child abuses. Some have physical problems resulting from the mistakes of ignorant or neglectful parents. Those born with fetal alcohol syndrome may never do well in school. Some children have received head injuries inflicted by angry parents or other caregivers that may affect their ability to learn. Others had such a poor diet in the early months critical to mental development that they may never learn normally. Others had tough toddler years that left the child with trust issues, anger, and defiance. Both male and female children may have been raped or sodomized. Beyond the physical damage, emotional attachment problems may be caused by any of these abuses.

Child abuse and neglect cross all ethnic, social, and economic lines. The consequences affect us all. "Child abuse leads to other problems such as long-term health and mental health problems, drug addiction, running away, juvenile violence, and adult crime. Most violent prisoners in our jails were abused or neglected as children."[8]

It is a national problem with more than 2.5 million reports of child abuse made annually in the United States. Hundreds of deaths are child-abuse related.[9] In New York State alone more than seventy thousand children are abused and neglected every year. Almost one hundred of them die. Most are less than five years old.[10]

Perhaps sexual abuse is what comes to mind most readily when we think of child abuse. It may take the form of fondling or touching the child's sexual organs, or making the child touch an adult sexually. Sexual abuse may include actual or attempted sexual intercourse or rape. In addition to the emotional trauma, this can produce severe physical injury to a young child. Children may be beaten as part of sexual activity. Forcing a child to take part in pornographic activities or to become part of a sex ring or child prostitution are other forms of sexual abuse of children.[11]

What physical signs or behaviors may indicate sexual abuse? In addition to sudden behavior changes such as Sally and Ed observed in their daughter, as a parent or caregiver for a young child, what should you look for? Torn, stained, or bloody underclothing are cause for alarm. If the child seems to have difficulty walking or sitting, or has pain or itching in the genital area, including bruises or bleeding, do your best to get more information from the child.

Of course, if signs of sexually transmitted disease or pregnancy appear, all doubt is removed. You must take action to find out who was involved and what may still be going on.

Behavioral indicators of sexual abuse may include unwillingness to change clothes or take part in gym classes at school. Sudden difficulty with toilet habits or abrupt withdrawn, fantastic, or infantile behavior may be clues.[12] If the child tells you of a sexual assault, praise the child for telling you. Believe the child. Find out as much as possible about the incident, but do so without pressuring the child. Don't ask the child to go over and over details of what happened. Keep the atmosphere calm no matter how angry or frightened you may be. Do not blame or punish the child. Reassure the child that you are there to protect him or her.[13] Immediately contact a physician to treat physical injuries the child may have. Take appropriate action to identify the abuser and stop the abuse. If the abuser is someone within the child's family or household, report it to the appropriate agency in your town. It may be called Child Protective Services, or Child Abuse Prevention, or a similar name. Look in the section of the telephone book for state and/or city offices. If the abuser is someone outside the family and household, report it to the local or state police or to the local sheriff's department.[14]

A word of caution should be added. Children with attachment issues may find it serves their purposes to lie about having been abused. A child may come to school with bruises gotten from falling out of a tree or even self-inflicted, but the story he or she gives the teacher is that "My mom hit me." The teacher is required to report this to law enforcement personnel, a fact the child almost certainly knows. More than one person who was not guilty has gone to jail for child abuse. The child made it up. Remember, unattached children feel the need to be in control. This is one of the keys to parenting a child with reactive attachment disorder (RAD). You, the grandparent or major caregiver, must take control and maintain it. Kids who have been removed from their birth parents or who have lived in many foster homes have been through so much trauma that they do not care about you or anything else, including the truth.

As previously pointed out, parenting techniques that work with children born into loving homes who have never been neglected or abused may not work with the tough little survivors of abuse and neglect who figure they have nothing to lose. And lying about it may be a fun way to get the adoptive dad or grandma or other caregiver in trouble so that the child remains in control. This is covered in chapter 4.

That being said, it is better to err on the side of believing the child's report until you are absolutely sure of what happened. The most unexpected persons sometimes abuse children.

Children who have been abused often keep it a secret. Some of their reasons are

- Fear of upsetting or disappointing parents or grandparents, or other caregivers.
- Embarrassment, especially about sexual abuse. If the child says nothing after the first encounter, he or she may be afraid or embarrassed to mention it after subsequent abuses.
- The abuser may threaten to harm the child or his or her family if he or she tells. An abuser may say something like "If you tell anybody, I'll kill your puppy."
- The abuser may tell the child it is a "game" or "This is okay. After all, I'm your uncle"—or cousin, neighbor, or friend. The child has been taught to respect and obey adults, so he or she says nothing.

Adults should understand how children are likely to communicate news of abuse. They may tell parts of what happened, or they may tell an adult that the activity happened to somebody else. A child may even tell you that he or she does not like to be alone with Mr. Smith or Uncle Joe. They are testing to see how the adult responds. If you respond negatively, accuse the child of lying, or respond emotionally and show extreme anger, the child will stop talking and probably not mention it again.

Adults or older children who wish to sexually abuse a young child may

- Insist on hugging, tickling, kissing the child when the child does not want the attention.
- Frequently offer to baby-sit or take children overnight
- Create ways to spend time alone with the child.
- Spend most of their spare time with children and have little interest in adult company.[15]

Grandparents who take over as primary caregivers for their grandchild may assume that the possibility of abuse has ended. However, they do well to recall the old adage "Forewarned is forearmed." It is well to be aware of how a child may act if he or she is being abused. It is wise to be alert to the "sideways" methods a child may use in trying to tell you about abuse in his or her past. It is prudent to know what to do if the child in your care has been or may be abused. Find out before any trouble begins what you should do if you learn a child is being sexually abused.

The best way to reduce the risk of abuse is to keep communication open with your grandchild. Teach children in your care about their bodies, what abuse is, and about sex. Teach them that it is your job to keep them safe but that you can protect them only if they tell you when something is wrong. Make it clear that no one has the right to touch them in a way that makes them uncomfortable.[16]

You can help prevent the sexual abuse of children in your care in several ways.

- Discuss sexuality in an open and honest way.
- Teach children to say no to someone who wants to touch sexual parts of their bodies.
- Be alert for clues that may signal abuse.

- Let children know they can speak openly with you. They don't need to keep bad secrets just because some adult asked the child to do so.
- Listen carefully. The child may not speak directly about sexual abuse.
- Know where your children are at all times and who they are with.
- Ask your child about what happens when he or she is alone with baby-sitters and others.
- Monitor what your children see on television and on the Internet. With whom are they communicating?[17]

Teach children what to do if a stranger approaches them with offers of gifts, a ride, or so on.

- Get away!
- Say no and yell for help.
- Run for help.
- Tell an adult as soon as possible.

If, in spite of your best efforts a child in your care is abused, assure him or her that it wasn't his or her fault.

Sharon Bryson, Director of Field Education for an academic social work program, believes much learning disability is a misdiagnosis. Bryson thinks that frequently the child's problem is undiagnosed sexual abuse. Bryson says changes in behavior to watch for include a child's tendency to set fires, to hurt animals, such as drowning a puppy or other small animal in the toilet. As he or she gets older, does he or she dress in black to be invisible? Does he or she gain weight to become unattractive?[18]

We began this chapter with the true story of Allyn, whose sexual abuse at the age of eight by a friend of her family destroyed her ability to have a normal life.

Born into a stable, two-parent, upper-middle-class family, Allyn had an angry childhood that was followed by drug addiction, the birth of a child out of wedlock whom she could not parent, and finally, life on the streets. Was that abuse the reason her life turned out so differently from that of her two sisters? No one knows. But it couldn't have helped.

Her parents blamed themselves for not recognizing the symptoms of sexual abuse. They probably were too hard on themselves, but Allyn's experience does point up the importance of staying alert to the possibility of such things happening to a child in your care. This is especially true if the child lived in the first years of his or her life with neglectful, perhaps drug-addicted parents. He or she may have undergone severe trauma of several kinds, including sexual abuse, before coming to you. Parenting methods may need to be modified accordingly.

Without help from a loving, concerned adult, a child probably cannot deal with the physical damage from abuse, much less the emotional distress. As the caregiver, if you become aware of unresolved issues stemming from past abuse, don't ignore them. The time to deal with the lingering hurts of sexual—or any—abuse is as soon as possible after it happens. Talk about it. Get professional help if necessary.

One sad outcome is the adult abused as a little child who never deals with it. The hurt simmers as he or she grows up but is repressed. Outwardly he or she appears to have no psychological problems. If such a person marries, he or she as well as the spouse may both be surprised to find that he or she has trouble forming a lasting relationship or responding to any bond. An adult who was abused as a child may even have flashbacks or symptoms of post-traumatic stress disorder. This applies to persons of either sex.

Grandparents or other caregivers must walk a tightrope of sorts. Nobody wants to find a danger behind every little bush. On the other hand, no child should have to suffer abuse without adult intervention to stop it. Being aware of the symptoms and keeping lines of communication open between you and the child are good starting points. Surely keeping a child safe from abusers should be a matter of prayer for all believing caregivers, remembering, as David said, "The Lord's unfailing love surrounds the man who trusts in him" (Psalm 32:10).

God still heals.

God, keep me alert and give me insight
as I watch over this child.

Questions for Support Group Discussion

1. Discuss the changes in behavior that may indicate a young child is being sexually abused.

2. Discuss the physical signs that a young child is being sexually abused.

3. Discuss ways you can help children in your care learn to protect themselves from sexual abuse.

seven

FOSTER CARE OR GRANDPARENT CARE?

Are you a grandparent who became a parent again when your child and his or her partner failed at parenting? Are you a grandparent who stepped up and took your grandchild in? Now, with full parental responsibility for one or more grandchildren, are you wondering if it was necessary? Was it worth the effort? *Am I making a difference? Wouldn't the children have been as well off in foster care?* If you are discouraged with what you have undertaken, read on. This chapter is for you. Like all the case histories in this book, what follows is each a true story.

"Back then you stayed in the hospital a week when you had a baby," said Pat. "I had a little girl. I named her Tabatha Michelle. When she was two days old, I was sitting there holding her when the nurse came in. She said, 'I'll take her now. She's not your baby any more.' She took Tabatha right out of my arms. I asked the nurse what she meant. The nurse said, 'The people who are adopting her are here.' She started out of the room. I don't know why I done it, but I grabbed a glass water pitcher sitting there and threw it at that woman."

"Nobody had asked you about putting the baby up for adoption?" I asked.

"They never said nothing. After I threw that pitcher—missed her—they come in and gave me a pill. Kept giving me pills. Kept me in la-la land until I got out of the hospital. I remember them taking me to court one day. I remember seeing that judge sitting up there. But I was so full of them pills I don't remember anything about what the judge said. Three weeks later Tabatha was adopted out. They named her something else."

"How old were you?"

"Fourteen."

"Fourteen! You had a baby at fourteen?"

"Yeah. I had it in my head that Tabatha and I were going home to our own little place."

"Who in the world was the father? Somebody you went to school with?" I asked.

Pat quit picking at the plate of liver and onions she had ordered with enthusiasm half an hour before. Her eyes met mine across the lunch table and held.

"Don't tell me it was the foster father? The guy who hit you with the cane?"

"Uh-huh. It was the foster father. I never told anybody."

"Why didn't you tell somebody?"

"Scared. He's dead now anyway."

"But it might have saved another girl from the same thing."

Pat ignored me. She sounded as if she were dictating oral history. "I was in a bunch of foster homes in those days. After my run-in with that foster father, they moved me to another foster home. Then moved me again right away to a home for unmarried mothers when they found out I was pregnant. This one was right next door to the insane asylum on Fourth Street in Lexington. They found him."

"How?" I asked.

"They calculated when she was conceived until the time she was born, and that's how they found him."

"Did anything happen to him?"

"He went to jail."

"For what? Child abuse?"

"Rape. He died in jail."

"Good," I said. I couldn't help myself.

More than 500,000 children in the United States are in foster care, a figure that has risen sharply in the last ten years. Ninety percent more children are in foster care now than in 1987.[1] Foster care refers to placement of a child under the age of eighteen with adults, usually unrelated to the child, who are paid to take parental responsibility. Social workers are responsible for seeing to it that children are not abused or neglected and for making the placements. They are employees of a state agency—Child Protective Services or some other name depending on your state. Most children who are placed temporarily in foster care are removed from the natural parents because of drug or alcohol abuse. Other reasons for foster placement include the parents having been sent to prison, the parents having abandoned the child, the parents suffering from physical or mental illness or death, or the parents having AIDS.[2] As noted earlier, sometimes grandparents or other relatives take in children with whom they have a blood-kin relationship on a foster care arrangement. Called "kinship care," the state pays the relatives as if they were unrelated foster parents. The state retains control of the child in these cases as it does in foster care by unrelated persons.

Although we can hope Pat's experience in foster care is unusual, such stories are common enough to raise disturbing suspicions. She told me about the home she was living in when she became pregnant.

"The people from Social Services placed me in that foster home. It was out in the country. The people ran a pig farm.

I've slopped hogs and delivered many a little pig. Every time the church door opened we were there, which was fine with me. I enjoyed the church services. It was what went on in the home." She gazed over my shoulder as she remembered.

"You know," she said, "one afternoon me and Linda—that was one of the other foster children—was sitting in the yard and our foster dad come out there with his cane and hit me across the back with it. I don't know what made me do it, but I said, 'If this is being very religious then you ain't religious.' I took that cane and hit him right across his head with it. I took off running across that field. By the time I got to the main road, the state police were there and took me to jail. I said I'd rather be in jail than go back there."

"The police believed him and not you?" I asked.

"They saw the welt on my back, but they didn't do nothing to him. They said 'You foster kids are problem kids anyway, or you wouldn't be in foster care.'"

"You didn't tell them your daddy drowned when you were six and the state took the five of you to foster care because your mom was always drunk?"

"Wouldn't have made any difference. They took me to another foster home. That's when they found out I was pregnant. They moved me again right away to the home for unmarried mothers."

From the time she went into foster care at age six until she aged out of the system at eighteen, Pat says she believes she was in nine or ten foster homes; she's lost count. She is now fifty-six years old, four children and three husbands later. She has found her eldest birth child, the little girl she called Tabatha. With the tacit approval of the adoptive parents, who named her Helen, she and Pat are in touch regularly. Pat counts Tabatha's/Helen's children as her own grandchildren.

Frequent moves are typical in foster care. Foster children on average live in three or four different foster homes. In many cases a foster child will have lived in over ten homes before they age out of the system or are returned to parents or grandparents. Many foster parents care for three to six foster children in their home at one time.[3]

In some cases action must be taken quickly to remove a child from his or her home in order to avoid injury to the child. In crisis situations a distinction is made between foster care and shelter care. Someone calls the police—perhaps late at night—to report that a child is in danger. The police or a social worker responds, removing the child from the home. The agency calls a relative if they can find one, or the agency may call specially trained and certified local foster parents to say there is a child in need of immediate housing. This is "shelter care." *Shelter care* is short-term care until more permanent arrangements can be made. If grandparents or other relatives can be located, they are usually offered the first opportunity to take the child.[4]

This type of crisis intervention is what happened to Carrie one sweltering July night. The twelve-year-old was alone with her sister, Maria, in the Los Angeles housing project apartment they called home. Their mother telephoned from a bar in the next block.

"Get out of the house," she said to Carrie. "I want you gone when I get home."

"When I saw her staggering across the bridge, I got scared and flagged down a passing police car," Carrie told me. "I told them if they left me with her, she would kill me. They didn't believe me. Instead, they took me to the door. My mother told one of the officers I was an incorrigible brat and she couldn't do anything with me. None of that was true. The policemen said, 'Now honey, you just go upstairs and lock the door and wait for Mommy to sober up.' As soon as the policemen left, my mother sent my sister to hold the door to keep me from running out. She came back with a strap. I shoved Maria out of the way and ran out. It was 3 A.M. I ran to the neighbors' house, and one of them called the police."

This time she was taken to juvenile hall and booked as a runaway. Only after Carrie recited to staff members at juvenile hall the names of the police officers who had failed to help her at the outset and told them what happened that night did they believe her story of her mother's intended violence.

Put into emergency shelter care at 5 A.M. that same early morning, Carrie was in three foster homes from July to October. Then her grandparents stepped in. She lived with them for several years. Her mother's parental rights were never legally terminated. Thus she was never available for adoption.

In Carrie's case, that was a shame.

"In one of the foster homes I was in, the lady—my foster mother for about two months—fell in love with me," Carrie says. "She and her husband wanted to adopt me. But my mother found out where I was. One day she called. I don't know what she said to me, but I screamed, ran out of the house, down past the pool, past the cabana——these people were really rich—on out into the woods where I cried for an hour. Then I came back into the house. Next time my mother called, Susan, my foster mother, picked up the phone and said, 'I have never seen a child so hurt. Don't you ever call her again.' She just advocated for me like that. As much as my mother hurt me, I remember actually feeling sorry for my mother that day. All these years later I still remember the foster mother's loving defense of me."

Pat's experience and Carrie's are the extremes of what can happen to a child in foster care. As in most of life, somewhere between the two extremes is probably the more common experience of foster children. We should note that there are reports that indicate that children die as a result of abuse in foster care 5.25 times more often than children in the general population.[5]

Often overlooked is that each move is traumatic for the child. Although many foster care cases originate when social workers try to get a youngster out of an unhealthy or dangerous situation, this is not how it appears to the child. From the child's viewpoint, strangers come in and yank him or her away from the only home the child has ever known, only to dump him or her in a place that is strange with people who are strangers. No wonder children who have experienced this upheaval conclude they must fend for themselves no matter what these new adults say or how well intentioned they sound.

Foster care is intended as a short-term arrangement until one of three permanent plans can be set in motion.

The first option is the child's reunification with the birth parents in the home when the state decides conditions are suitable. This is what everyone hopes will happen.

The second plan is put in motion when the foster home becomes the permanent home and the birth parents' parental rights are terminated and the foster parents become permanent legal guardians or, in many cases, adopt the child as their own.

The third outcome is guardianship or long-term care in a foster home. This sometimes happens, as it did in Carrie's case, when the child cannot be reunited with his or her birth family but adoption is not an option.[6]

Sometimes birth parents voluntarily place their child in foster care. The parent or parents may be unwilling or unable to care for the child. If the child has behavioral problems that require treatment beyond the skills of the birth family, he or she may be placed with specially trained foster parents. This is referred to as therapeutic parenting or therapeutic foster care.

Child Protective Services, or whatever the agency is called in the state where you reside, maintains legal control of children who are in foster care. The state pays foster parents to care for the child. Reimbursement rates in many states are lower than the actual costs of providing routine care for a child.[7]

The median age of children in foster care in a recent year was 10.2 years. Two out of three children in foster care can be reunited with birth parents within two years. Reports vary on who the 510,000 children were in foster care in 2006. Some studies have found about two-thirds of the children in foster care are African-American. These same studies find that African-American children tend to remain in foster care longer than those of other ethnic groups.[8] Another study finds that forty percent of the children in foster care were white/non-Hispanic. Thirty-two percent were black, non-Hispanic; nineteen percent Hispanic; and nine percent were other races or multiracial. To have slightly more boys than girls in foster care has been a consistent trend in the United States. In 2006, fifty-two percent of foster children were male, forty-eight percent female.[9]

The result of a recent study on what becomes of foster children when they become eighteen years old and must leave foster care is discouraging. Three in ten of the nation's homeless are former foster children. A recent study has found that twelve to eighteen months after leaving foster care, twenty-seven percent of the males and ten percent of the females had been incarcerated, thirty-three percent were receiving public assistance, thirty-seven percent had not finished high school, and fifty percent were unemployed.[10] Child abuse and neglect occur at about the same rate in all racial and ethnic groups.[11]

In spite of the discouraging stories of abuse, many foster parents are unselfish men and women who provide the care because they love children. They open their homes and hearts to children in need of temporary care. The task is rewarding but difficult.

"You just love 'em, honey," says North Carolina adoptive parent Trina. Trina and her husband, David, have had thirty-seven children stay with them. Of these, they have adopted six, now ranging in age from four to eighteen. Five of these six were expected to be reunited with their biological families when Trina and David took them into their home. When it was clear that reunification was impossible and the children's birth parents' rights were terminated, they were free to adopt them and did so.[12]

Sometimes foster children know you love them by the tone of your voice. Pat, the woman impregnated at age fourteen by her foster father, tells of another foster home to which she was assigned.

"I'd get uptight and threaten to run away. My sweet foster mother would say, 'Well, Pat, there's the road. But it might get chilly tonight. Better take a sweater.'"

"Was calling your bluff a good approach?" I asked.

"It wasn't so much that," Pat said, "as the way she said it. I just knew she loved me. Her eyes were so soft and her voice just had a tone that let me know she cared about me. She wanted only good things for me."

"Fosterage," as the practice of a family bringing up a child not their own is called, has been in use for centuries. Originally it had nothing to do with the natural parents' inability to raise their child. Rather, it was seen as a way for influential families to cement political relationships. In Scotland in the eighteenth century "fosterage" was used in this way. A man of wealth and prominence might send his child, either male or female, to his tenant or to a distant friend to be fostered. To be requested to foster a child was considered an honor and a trust. The father sent with his child a number of cows. The fosterer added the same number. The fathers established terms for pasturing the cows and how any calves were to be divided, some returning with the child. Children stayed with the fostering family for perhaps six years. The friendships thus developed were thought to have good effects.[13] The foster care of that day was rather like an arranged marriage, made not because the parties loved each other but for strengthening a political alliance between two families. It may even have been used to improve diplomatic relations between nations. The child's emotional needs were almost certainly not considered. Today foster care refers entirely to being paid by a government agency to bring up a child not your own because of the failure or inability of the natural parents to do so.

Just as children often blame themselves for their parents' divorce, children placed in foster care may blame themselves and feel guilty because a stranger from the government thought it necessary to intervene and separate them from their natural parents.

"Children in foster care are three to six times more likely than children not in foster care to have emotional, behavioral, and developmental problems, including conduct disorders, depression, difficulties in school, and impaired social relationships. Some experts estimate that about thirty percent of the children in care have marked or severe emotional problems. Various studies have indicated that children and young people in foster care tend to have limited education and job skills, perform poorly in school compared to children who are not in foster care, lag behind in their education by at least one year, and have lower educational attainment than the general population."[14] Another study found that eighty percent of prison inmates have been through the foster care system.[15]

The jokes about wanting nothing in life but a little white house with a picket fence around it appear to have basis in fact. Children do better in stable, two-parent homes, secure and loved, with the brief years of childhood untroubled by adult concerns they don't understand.

If you, a grandparent, have intervened in your grandchild's life to make it more secure, remember that you are making a vast difference. If you think what you are doing doesn't matter, think again. Well-intentioned as many foster homes are, a loving home with people related by blood with whom the children are at least somewhat acquainted is better.

"But I don't have the strength to continue at my age," grandparents sometimes say. Remember who the real source of strength is. The Bible says, "My help comes from the LORD, the maker of heaven and earth" (Psalm 121:2). "God is our refuge," adds Psalm 62:8. If you are raising a second set of children, ask the Lord to make real to you His words through the psalmist:

O my Strength, I sing praise to you; you, O God, are my fortress, my loving God *(Psalm 59:17)*.

Children from homes affected by their parents' drug and alcohol use have already known abuse and neglect. If you, a grandparent or other relative, can possibly avoid it, do not add the distress of frequent shuffling among foster homes to the child's burden. See what your loving care can mean.

God never loses sight of anyone.

Lord, help me help this child
during this time of transition.

Questions for Support Group Discussion

1. Ninety percent more children are in foster care now than twenty years ago. Discuss the reasons for that.

2. Do the grandparents in your group feel that taking on the responsibility of raising their grandchildren is superior to the children being placed in foster care? Why or why not?

3. If grandparents in your group feel they have taken on more than they can handle, discuss ways they can find help.

eight

DID I CAUSE THIS MESS?
ENABLING AND BLAME

"Well, good. That's taken care of," Hannah said to her daughter, Shirley, as she hung up the phone.

"What's taken care of?" asked Shirley.

"Greg and Sarah, of course. I couldn't sleep nights knowing those poor babies were living in their car. I went over to Longwood Apartments the other day and made arrangements for them to have a nice one-bedroom for six months. They should be on their feet by then. The manager just called to say their place is ready. They can move in any time."

"Mother, this has got to stop!" Shirley was practically screaming.

"I thought Christians were supposed to think of others. How can you abandon your own child?"

"I'm not abandoning anybody."

"You most certainly are. They wouldn't even have an automobile if I hadn't gotten them another one after their accident."

"Accident? Greg totaled it driving drunk. He'd still be in jail if you hadn't bailed him out, another one of your well-meant disasters."

"Shirley! Don't talk like that. I'm your mother."

Greg, Hannah's grandson, is twenty-six years old, the oldest of Shirley and Richard's three children. He and his girlfriend, Sarah, have been together six years and have two children. In the last year they have lost their house, their car, and their children to their drug and alcohol addictions. Local authorities removed the kids from their home after determining the children were severely neglected. Ultimately the state terminated their parental rights. Now the children, four-year-old Jordan and his one-year-old sister, Jewel, live with Shirley and Richard, who are in the process of adopting them. Richard is fifty-five years old; Shirley is fifty-three.

Greg and Sarah show no inclination to seek treatment for their addictions nor do they show interest in parenting their children. They express no remorse that their one-year-old has been diagnosed with fetal alcohol syndrome and the accompanying limited intellectual capacity and its identifying features.

Grandmother Hannah to the rescue! Hannah, Shirley's mother, lives with Shirley and Richard in their home. Hannah means well, but no one has been able to convince her that paying for leases on apartments for Greg and Sarah isn't helping them. The car she gave them after Greg's accident while driving drunk is just one of several automobiles she has supplied them. The other cars have been demolished in similar drunk-driving accidents, with the exception of one that was destroyed by vandals while Greg and Sarah were living in it in a dangerous area of town.

Greg is quite personable when sober. He visits his parents' home frequently and tells his grandmother what a great lady she is. He swears that if she will just loan him enough money to get through this month, he will never touch booze again. With memories of the sweet little boy Greg was and being in denial about his addictions, Hannah believes his lies. She covers for him when necessary, continues to give him money—she calls it giving him *loans*—and repeatedly signs leases on apartments for him and Sarah.

Grandmother Hannah is enabling Greg. It's called *enabling*, because it enables Greg to continue his destructive behavior. Greg and Sarah are shielded from accepting responsibility of the consequences of their addictions and their conduct.

Are you inclined to enable people you love to continue with bad behavior? Or is your life being affected by someone you love who is enabling another? Christians may be especially vulnerable to the temptation to enable wrong behavior because they read in their Bibles that they should be compassionate. They are told to feed the hungry and care for the poor. They also read that those who do not care for their own families are worse than unbelievers. According to 1 Timothy 5:8, KJV, they are worse than "infidels." Torn between what they see as a Christian duty to those who are less fortunate and the nagging idea that bailing a drunk out of jail three months in a row isn't smart, kindhearted people like Hannah struggle between enabling and letting the addict finally hit bottom. When at last there is no place to look but up, perhaps the person will seek the only real source of lasting help—God's forgiveness, grace, and strength.

Grandparents raising their children's children should be prepared to confront two emotions: guilt and the temptation to enable. *Am I to blame for my child's failure? What did I do wrong?* It's a short step from there to the idea that if you help just a little bit, he or she will surely beat the addictions. Enabling often begins as an honest, well-meaning attempt to be helpful and kind.

Enabling can be defined as actions that, while done with good intentions, have the effect of rescuing the person from the consequences of his or her own bad behavior, actions that enable the person to continue to engage in behaviors that are destructive to self or others.[1]

Grandmother Hannah gave Greg and Sarah the rent money in cash one month. She was astonished that they spent it on drugs and alcohol and wound up still living on the street. She thought it was unchristian of her daughter and son-in-law to refuse to let Greg and Sarah move in with them until they got things straightened out.

Hannah's idea of correcting the problem was to pay the landlord herself. Greg and Sarah never got their hands on the money, and it would keep them in the apartment for a few more months.

Hannah is unable to admit to herself that she is part of Greg and Sarah's problem. They continue to take advantage of her naiveté. Shielded from the consequences of their behavior, they continue destructive habits.

Sometimes an enabler becomes frustrated and angry when he or she sees that these enabling efforts are ineffective. But not Grandmother Hannah! She doesn't realize it, but her solution to her grandson's problem is to deny that it is happening. She refuses to see the truth because to do so would be painful. She would have to admit that her beloved grandchild is failing at life. Besides, if she didn't help Greg, he might be angry and not like her any more. From Hannah's enabler perspective, she sees herself somehow responsible for her grandson's problems.

Hannah may be correct about the anger. Greg probably wouldn't like it if his free money stopped. Enablers can never end their fruitless conduct until they realize that they are not responsible for the addict's behavior. Enablers must gather themselves, developing enough strength and pride to take a stand, and break their own destructive cycle of enabling behavior. Hannah must learn to say to herself that her money is hers, that Greg and Sarah are adults, capable of getting jobs and paying their own bills if they would. She is not responsible for them. She must see that they probably will not beat the addictions until they touch bottom and are forced to face the reality of their condition. She must face the sadness of admitting that her grandson is indeed wasting his life and her help is aiding him in doing so. She does not realize that she herself has a disease called "enabling" from which she needs to be healed. Until she quits making excuses for Greg, quits believing his lies, stops paying bills for which she is not responsible, stops making excuses for him to her friends, she will not recover.

Enabling behaviors do not usually disappear abruptly. The enabler must realize that he or she is in need of healing, just as the addict is. The enabler must see that his or her efforts to help are self-defeating, delaying, and hindering the recovery of the addict. Even after an enabler begins to identify the behaviors that are unhelpful and make changes, such understanding probably will come gradually.

How can it be done? In Hannah's case, if her daughter, Shirley, and her husband could convince Hannah to go with them to a support group like Al-Anon, she would meet other persons with the same circumstances. Hearing their stories might give her a more objective view of her own behavior. She might find herself identifying with other Al-Anon members. Perhaps she would gain insight into her own behavior by discussing it with a person from her generation who does not know Greg and has no emotional connection with the family.

Another possible approach is for Shirley to offer to go with her mother to see a Christian therapist or counselor who specializes in the problems of addiction. The counselor could provide insight into the nature of addiction in terms Hannah would accept. Perhaps Shirley could persuade her mother to go by saying the counselor could show her better ways to help her grandson. Over time we can hope Hannah would come to see her true condition and stop the enabling.

Grandparents raising their child's children may be an enabler of the misbehaving child in a more subtle way than Hannah. Hannah, you notice, is one more generation removed from the little children whose care has changed life forever for Richard and Shirley. If, instead, you are the grandparent—the Richard and Shirley in this actual case history—with full parental responsibility for your child's children, it is almost a given that you will be overextended physically, emotionally, and usually financially. If you are too exhausted at the end of each day to care anymore, it's easy to justify doing the simplest thing rather than what is best for the grandchild or his or her parent. Struggling with physical and emotional exhaustion, sometimes still laboring under a burden of guilt, you are caring for grandchildren while listening to your failed child's plea for help on his or her terms and at his or her convenience. In such a case, it's easy to become your drunk/addicted/jailed child's banker and lawyer. Some grandparents become their adult child's secretary and administrative assistant, his or her insurance and bond company. In other words, they take over responsibility and continue to support this failed adult.

Most of all, parents risk becoming their child's protector, says Gene Doyle, a Lexington, Kentucky, graphic artist and advertising executive who teaches seminars for parents with problem children.[2] He and his wife, Karen, became family counselors after dealing with their own children's drug and alcohol abuse. Doyle developed a curriculum that he teaches regularly to help parents with out-of-control children and grandparents coping with raising their children's children.

Doyle says grandparents raising their grandchildren tend to defend and support their child, the grandchild's parent, no matter what he or she has done. It's a short step from there to taking the blame for any bad decision the child makes. Whether they deserve blame or not, they take it. They're too tired to sort it out and do anything else. They figure this mess must be their fault. Their son is in jail on drug charges. His girlfriend, their grandchild's mother, is a drunk. And the whole thing is their fault. They must have been bad parents. The least they can do is bail him out of jail one more time, pay for one more round of rehab, pay rent on his apartment for six months—again—when they discover that he and the girlfriend are living in their car. They believe they should do all of this because they're Christians, and they should help those who are down on their luck. Right?

Wrong!

"Believe you me," says Doyle, "such persons will let you support them as long as you will take the responsibility and spend your money." Christians who impulsively want to help a person down on his or her luck combined with the natural emotions generated by having to take over the children of their child who has failed miserably can quickly motivate enabling behavior.

How does one tell the difference between rescuing and enabling? When does helping your child turn into hurting your child? How does one keep his or her understandable emotions of sadness and guilt from being completely overwhelming?

One test is this, Doyle says: Is your child making good decisions? You can help the child who is making good decisions. If he or she has profited from rehab, if he or she is clean from drugs, if he or she has a regular job, then maybe you are really helping and not enabling to let him or her live with you for a few months until he or she can pay rent on a place in a safe neighborhood.

What you can't do is help the child who is making poor decisions. If he or she is still addicted, behaving irresponsibly, letting him or her move in with you, paying his or her rent, fixing the car, and things like that become enabling. It becomes *your child's* freedom at *your* expense. It is enabling, and it is the wrong thing to do.

Doyle points to the distinction Paul made between true helpfulness and weakening aid in his letter to the Galatians. Galatians 6:2 says, "Carry each other's burdens." Grandparents who mean to help their wrong-headed children sometimes read that far and stop, Doyle says. They don't read on down to Galatians 6:5, which says, "For each one should carry his own load." Doyle points out that the original Greek word Paul uses in verse 2 means to help others with excessive hardship. It is the same word Jesus used when He said, "Come to me, all you who are weary and burdened, and I will give you rest" (Matthew 11:28). Help the person who is doing the best he or she can but is going down under the load. The Greek word in the other place, Galatians 6:5, means that each of us should carry his or her own cargo, shoulder his or her own backpack, and take responsibility for his or her own daily chores and duties. Most of all, we are responsible for our own sins.

It is worth noting that a couple of verses down the page beyond the verses quoted above, Paul observes, "God cannot be mocked. A man reaps what he sows" (Galatians 6:7). If you think God doesn't see through your motives, Paul says you're deceiving yourself. Paul says that if we sow to please our "sinful nature," we will reap destruction. He goes on to say in verse 8 that if we sow "to please the Spirit," we "will reap eternal life."

Some situations are exceptions to the rules about enabling. These apply to the child or grandchild still living under the parents' or grandparents' roof. While Doyle is entirely aware of the destructive effects of enabling, he says that there are four situations that are not to be viewed as enabling. They are so serious that parents and grandparents should get professional help as soon as they become aware of the behavior. For a younger child who is still living with you, in these four situations you should not look away. Early intervention on behalf of a young child may prevent a bigger problem later. You are not enabling when you take prompt action in the following four circumstances, Doyle says.

The child runs away from home. Even if he or she just goes away overnight to somebody's house and doesn't let you know, it means something deeper is happening in the child's life that is beyond what you know. You are seeing only the tip of the iceberg, and the child needs professional help.

Nancy Thomas, therapeutic parenting specialist, says there are times when the parent or grandparent must install alarms on the child's bedroom door and the windows of his or her room. This is especially true of children with attachment problems or who have been abused or neglected early in life. Many children who are being raised by grandparents come from early childhood trauma severe enough to produce attachment difficulties. Explain to the child why you are installing the alarms. He or she will test the door alarm. It will disturb your sleep, but you will become aware of his or her activities at night, and this will empower you.[3]

The child steals. The child may become guilty of stealing from friends or others, stealing or shoplifting items from a store, or stealing from you. As a parent or grandparent, the child is doing something with the money that he or she doesn't want you to know about. A secretive lifestyle is going on. The child needs help. So do you. Don't leave purses or billfolds in easy-to-find places. Never keep large sums of cash around the house, and hide what money you do have. Be sure credit or debit cards are hidden in a secure spot as well.

The child is abusing drugs or alcohol or is physically or verbally abusing siblings or parents. The same rule applies to grandparents with full parental responsibility for young grandchildren. If the kid is always in your face, cursing you, you have a problem serious enough to justify professional help. Children with attachment problems should not be allowed to have a pet until their hearts are healed. They may torture or kill the pet. They may also do things such as cut the legs off stuffed animals or set fires.

Any talk of death or suicide. Take this kind of talk seriously, and get professional help.

Doyle says that any one of these four things is a warning sign of a child in danger. It means you, as a grandparent or parent, are in over your head. Don't wait—get help as quickly as possible. The situation is beyond your ability to fix. You need to engage the services of a licensed Christian counselor, a psychiatrist, perhaps a pastor experienced in counseling persons in the age brackets of both you and your child or grandchild.

Frequent lying often goes hand-in-hand with these behaviors. Girls especially seem inclined to lie to their caregivers about where they are going, what they will be doing, and with whom they will be doing it. A child who lies to you has a secret lifestyle.

These behaviors are harbingers of worse things to come.

"Is there hope?" I asked Richard, who with his wife, Shirley, is raising their twenty-six-year-old son's two children. They continue to cope with Shirley's mother's misguided attempts to help their son and his girlfriend.

"There is always hope," he replies. "Greg was raised in a home where we served the Lord. We have a history of giving ourselves away to others. Is there hope? Absolutely, because we serve a God of hope."

He laughs. "Jordan and I both like amusement park rides. He's four now. We went to a local amusement park for his birthday and had a blast. We laughed a lot. I try not to be overwhelmed by thoughts of what will happen five or ten years from now. God is faithful. We trust him for the future as we have the past."

**If you seek God through His Word,
He will give you practical and useful advice.**

*Lord, help me stay strong and not enable
my child's destructive lifestyle.*

Questions for Support Group Discussion

1. If any in your group feel they are enablers of their adult children who cannot raise their own children, discuss how they became enablers.

2. Discuss what emotions or motivations cause enabling behaviors.

3. Are there members of your group who are beginning to realize they have enabling tendencies?

4. Discuss reasons it is difficult to break enabling habits.

5. Discuss ways enablers can get help that will allow them to allow their children to be responsible for their own behavior.

6. There are four childhood behaviors named in this chapter that should prompt grandparents to seek profession help. Discuss those behaviors, and invite input from any grandparents who have or are experiencing those behaviors in their grandchildren.

nine

EXPERIENCING GUILT

David and Margaret recall the day they went to court to get legal custody of their grandson after the state took him away from their drug-addicted daughter-in-law, Marlene. She tested positive on the routine drug test the hospital ran the day he was born.

The judge, dressed in a long black robe, every wave of his hair carefully in place, looked down from his high bench.

"Are you this boy's grandparents?"

"Yes, your honor—we are," said David.

"I grant you custody of your grandchild." Looking at Margaret, he added, "Try to do a better job this time."

"We knew we hadn't been perfect parents," said David, "but why the guilt trip? We raised all of our children alike, and we're not sure why our son has struggled so."

Was the judge being fair? If you are a grandparent raising your child's children, should you feel guilty? Are you to blame for your child's inability to parent his or her own child? Whether it is drug or alcohol addiction, incarceration, mental illness, or another reason, the effect is the same. You are reentering the parent game. At a time in life that you had hoped to be doing your own thing—traveling, playing a lot of golf, sleeping late—you are back on the school bus and homework circuit.

"When our son Timothy went to jail on drug charges and we realized we had to raise our grandson," says Margaret, "we went through a grief process because we had lost what we had planned for our lives. The mother is a drunk who cares very little about the child. When we brought Kenneth home from the hospital, two years ago now, it should have been the happiest day of our lives. He was our first grandchild. Instead, we grieved as if our son had died."

David and Margaret had planned to retire in their fifties and pursue new interests. Now, she says, they will be working into their seventies. "Sometimes I feel sad about that," Margaret says. "But then I look at little Kenny, the grandson we are raising, and it's all worth it."

Feeling guilt and failure is understandable. Perhaps it is even normal and to be expected. You raised your kids. You know you made some mistakes—what parent hasn't?—but on the whole you thought the home you provided was a pretty good one. You and your spouse loved the Lord and tried to seek His will in everything. You loved your children. You kept them fed and housed. They went to school and church. You taught all of them about Jesus. Why did one of them turn out so differently from the others? *What if. . . If only. . .*

If you're a grandparent raising your children's children, do *what if* and *if only* plague you?

Sometimes your child can answer that for you. David and Margaret, who are raising their son Timothy's young son, are college-educated, middle-class folks. Margaret taught in a local Christian high school until she became a stay-at-home mom—again—to care for her grandchild. David, a communications professional, recounts taking his son to lunch before he went to jail. Timothy showed up looking unusually good that day; he was sober and well dressed.

"I want my son back," David said to Timothy during lunch. "I love you, but I will not fund anything for you. I will not enable your drug habit in any way." David said Timothy seemed to understand. Timothy's parents had paid rent on several apartments. They had pleaded and reasoned and reminded him of what the Bible says about godly living. Nothing they had done had made a difference. David and Margaret realized further effort to rescue him would hinder, not help, Timothy's recovery.

At lunch that day David was suddenly overwhelmed with sadness. "I'm sorry, Tim. I failed you," he told his son.

Timothy looked up from his lunch. "No, you didn't, Dad. My lifestyle is my choice. You aren't responsible for the way I turned out. This is how I decided to live. They were my choices."

"Coming from our son, the meth addict, that was impressive," David remarked to me in an interview for this book. "I didn't give him credit for having that much perspective, much less a willingness to let me off the hook."

Scripture confirms what Timothy said. "The soul who sins is the one who will die. The son will not share the guilt of the father, nor will the father share the guilt of the son" (Ezekiel 18:20). This is the general teaching of the Bible. God sees us and loves each of us as individuals. But we are each ultimately responsible for what we do and for our response to God's love. See also Deuteronomy. 24:16; Jeremiah 31:30; Job 19:4; and Proverbs 9:12.

"Parents should not feel ashamed when they are having problems with their kids. Churches should send them the message that it is not their fault," says Gene Doyle, businessman who, with his wife, Karen, runs a Christian ministry called Parent Power. Doyle, whose advice I shared in an earlier chapter, teaches a class for parents and grandparents coping with problem children and young people. The ministry grew out of the Doyles' own parenting experience. Their trial ended happily; their wild-child son is now a responsible business executive, husband, and father. Doyle says,

God put Adam and Eve in a perfect environment, and they messed up. You are not a failure because your kids turn out wrong any more than God is a failure because His kids turned out wrong.

Does that mean God is a poor parent? Of course not. It means God created us with free will. Adam and Eve did their own thing. The sin was rebellion. They ate the forbidden fruit, and they believed Satan's lie.

Adam and Eve—and Timothy—made their own choices. Doyle believes that grandparents who are raising their grandchildren wait too long to get help. Support groups and seminars, such as the one Doyle leads, books, and professional Christian counselors all stand ready to help grandparents who are struggling with their children's behavior and the needy little grandchildren who often come to the grandparents as jaded survivors of abuse and neglect. He believes churches should teach parenting workshops to specifically address the unique problems grandparents face in raising grandchildren who have been through hard times early in life.

One unique problem that should be addressed early on is what the grandchildren will call the grandparents who are raising them. If the children are young enough they sometimes solve that dilemma on their own by calling their grandparents Mom and Dad. If they go with the standard Grandma and Grandpa or some derivative, they may have to answer awkward questions when they start preschool or school.

"Why are you different?" children ask. "Where's your mommy? Why do you live with your grandma?" These are difficult questions for a six-year-old who doesn't want to be unusual.

Another situation you may face is if the child in frustration over some discipline yells, "You're not my mom. I don't have to do what you say!" Grandparents should anticipate this problem and decide on a course of action before it becomes an issue.

Adam and Eve's story in Genesis informs us on parenting methods to some extent. God, having given His children free will, had to put up with their disobedience. But notice that at the outset God made His rules and standards clear. When the rules were broken, God did not dillydally. He fixed the punishment and carried it out. Things were clear-cut. See Genesis 3:14-19, 22-24. In dealing with children and grandchildren, pray for wisdom about what rules to set. Ask God for wisdom in setting a punishment and when to invoke that punishment. Ask Him to help you be merciful and compassionate while still being firm and consistent. Ask Him to show you how to know the difference between extending needed help and doing things that are enabling. If you ask Him, you can expect God to lead you to Christian friends or counselors who can help you.

The practical God who helped the prophet find a lost axe head in 2 Kings 6:5 and told the disciples where to cast a net to catch fish in John 21:6 will surely answer prayers about raising children. Notice also that when Adam and Eve disobeyed, God compassionately adapted His original plan to provide needed help and comfort for His children.

David says that in his head he knows that what his son told him that day at lunch is true: he is not responsible for the decisions of a twenty-six-year-old man. Yet his breaking heart cries out that he must have made mistakes in parenting that caused his son's behavior. In spite of much prayer and their best efforts, David and Margaret sometimes are overcome with guilt and great sadness. They think they must have been bad parents or this wouldn't have happened. They wondered if they failed to model Christian marriage correctly or if they were too hard on Timothy when he was little. He had accepted Christ when he was a youngster; did they fail to follow up somehow? Even Tim's siblings don't understand their brother. They wonder why Timothy is different. The whole family wonders if they unconsciously treated him differently. Sometimes

David and Margaret think that surely only bad parents could produce a child so dysfunctional that he can't raise his own child.

Variations on this story are played out in millions of American homes every day. According to a 2010 U.S. Census press release, two and a half million grandparents are raising about 5.7 million grandchildren with full parental responsibility. That is eight percent of all the children in the United States. Perhaps eighty to ninety percent of the cases arise because the parents are addicted to drugs and/or alcohol. In other cases the children's parents are in jail, are mentally ill, have AIDS, or have died.

"Parents who are in crisis with their kids all have the same emotions," says Gene Doyle. Through their ministry, Parent Power, he and his wife, Karen, deal with parents and grandparents like David and Margaret. "It's a deep sense of failure, a deep sense of self-blame, a deep sense of sadness," Doyle says. Doyle, who shared his insights on enabling drug and alcohol abusers in the previous chapter, meets this sense of failure head-on. "I take these grandparents right back to the Bible," Doyle says of his teaching method. "We start in Genesis, and I show grandparents how God was the perfect parent for Adam and Eve." Doyle makes the point that God put His first-created children in a perfect environment. The Garden of Eden was not a tenement slum. God did what parents are supposed to do: He talked with Adam and Eve, spent time with them every day. He gave them rules and consequences.

"As a matter of fact," says Doyle, "He didn't give them a whole lot of rules. He gave them just one: they were not to eat of the tree of good and evil. Failure to follow the rule would have consequences. What did they do? They broke the rule! The bottom line is you can be a perfect parent, put your child in a perfect environment, create rules and boundaries, and there still are no guarantees. And the reason there isn't a guarantee is because the child has that little quirky thing built in him or her that we all have. It's called freedom of choice. And like Adam and Eve, he or she is free to make his or her own choices, no matter how good the parenting."

"Here's the thing that parents do," Doyle says. "A lot of parents get stuck on this point. They think that if they have a bad kid, it must mean they're bad parents. And if they have good kids, they must be good parents. Well, it's absolutely false, because if that were the case, then you would have to say God was not a very good parent. Because His first kids, Adam and Eve, didn't turn out too well. You can't judge God's parenting based on these kids. Neither can you judge an imperfect parent who doesn't have the resources and capabilities that God does. They can't be judged on the outcome of their kids."

Doyle is quick to add that there are parents who are bad influences on their children, and this is a key point, Doyle believes. You are not responsible for how your child behaves, but you are responsible for the influence you give your child.

"God does not hold you responsible for what your kid does, but He holds you responsible for how you treat your kid," Doyle says. "Your job is to influence."

Doyle adds the caveat that your child must be *willing* to be influenced. "When it comes to teenage rebellion, the rubber meets the road. You may influence as much as you can, but they may not be willing to be influenced."

Doyle readily admits that this can lead to issues of rescuing or enabling. As a parent attempting to influence, ask yourself if you do things that actually enable a teenager's bad behavior to continue. What kind of rules and boundaries can you set that will bring about change in your teenager's life? At what point do you back away and allow your child to suffer the consequences of his or her bad choices?

Doyle sees two things that are agents of change: *pain and reward*. Are you using rules and boundaries to let the child in your care experience the negative consequences of bad behavior? Are you letting the child experience the rewards of good choices?

Parents may inadvertently corner themselves, Doyle believes, by taking credit for the good things their children do.

Somebody comes up to me and says, "Hey, Gene, how is your boy?" Well, of course I am going to say, "Oh, he's great. He's the first-string quarterback on the high school team." If they ask about my daughter, I'll say, "She's a piano prodigy." Or if they inquire about my elder son, I'm going to say, "He's an intellectual genius." Even though it may or may not be true, we put a good face on it. And because we put a good face on it, what we are doing is acting as our child's talent agent. We are taking credit for something that doesn't belong to us. What we need to be doing instead when somebody asks about the kid is say, "You know what? My kid is making some good choices for himself. I am just thrilled with the fact that he has chosen to study hard and pull his grades up. I am thrilled with how much work he has put into doing well on his ball team. But he is the one who deserves the credit for all that. I am the one who is just standing back and being happy about it."

You can see where this leads. If I start taking credit for my child's successes, guess what happens when my child fails? I start taking the blame. The whole thing comes down to how you talk to your kid, what kind of rules and boundaries you set, how you feel about your kid. You let the child take responsibility for making good choices or bad ones. All of these things fit together, you see.

Doyle agrees that grandparents raising their children's children may feel resentment as well as guilt and grief. Life was not easy for today's grandparents, he says. They often wanted to be certain that their children had an easier time of it than they had. The result has been that the middle generation—those who are now unable to parent their own children—were given much freedom in the first two decades of their lives. The problem was that many of those kids developed the mantra "My freedom at your expense." They never grew up, Doyle thinks. When their children came along, these parents were busy pleasing themselves. Often this meant drug and alcohol use.

All parents make mistakes with their children. But if you have made it clear by your actions that you love your child unconditionally, if you have humbly apologized to your child when you have made mistakes, if you have done the best you knew to do and have given your children good advice and been a positive influence in their lives, you have nothing for which to blame yourself. Doyle believes that you cannot cancel another person's free will. If your child made bad choices, is guilty of crimes, and sins against his or her own body and against others, then these were his or her decisions.

As a grandparent raising your grandchildren, you have a unique opportunity to improve your parenting techniques. It is a chance to change some of the practices you wish you had done differently in raising your own children.

Raising your children's children is a big job to take on. Don't make it even harder by carrying the heavy emotional freight of guilt because your children have failed in their duty as parents. It's not your fault. True, there may be some things you could have done better. Every parent can say that. But in the end, you are not responsible for the choices, good or bad, that another person makes.

It's been five years now since the judge publicly rebuked David and Margaret.

"When the state terminated our son's parental rights," said David, "and those of our grandson's mother, I said to Margaret, 'Let's just adopt him. Then nobody can ever take him away from us.'" That's what they did.

When I asked David, who is now 53, if he can keep up with an energetic, growing boy, he laughs and says, "I run marathons. I think I'll be able to jog a couple of miles every day with a youngster."

**Even God's first children, Adam and Eve,
were disobedient and made poor decisions.**

*Lord, release me from misplaced guilt,
and point me toward the hope I have in you.*

Questions for Support Group Discussion

1. Are there grandparents in your group who feel they're bitter toward their adult children who have failed at life, thus putting the grandparents in the position of having to raise their grandchildren? Discuss forgiveness.

2. Are their grandparents in your group who feel it is their failure as parents that caused an adult child to be unable to parent his or her own children? Discuss the issues of guilt discussed in this chapter.

3. Discuss guidelines mentioned in this chapter that will help grandparents establish rules and consequences for raising their grandchildren.

ten

FINANCING ANOTHER FAMILY

It has become so common for relatives other than the biological parents to raise children not their own that a term has been coined for it. "Grandfamily" refers to the family unit created when grandparents or other relatives are raising a child or children not their own to whom they are related by blood, marriage, or adoption. Such an arrangement is sometimes called *kinship care, kincare,* or *relative care.*[1]

Often when these families are established, money becomes a major consideration. Raising children is expensive. If you're a grandparent who has already raised one set of children, you are well aware of this financial fact. Now, as you set out to do it again, you're twenty or thirty years older and possibly retired and on a fixed income.

When it became apparent that your child was not going to adequately parent his or her children, you took on the responsibility. Maybe you didn't think about the cost then, but now you must.

When listing the matters that grandparents raising grandchildren worry about most, David Bassoni, Program Coordinator and Aging Planner for the Bluegrass Area Agency on Aging in Kentucky, says, "Money has got to be at the top of the heap. Not in the sense [that grandparents think] somebody ought to pay them to care for the child. But if they're on a fixed or low income, finances quickly push to the front of the worry list. Money is an issue for at least eighty percent of the grandparents we talk to." Food, clothing, and medical care require cash, and no amount of love helps meet those financial obligations.

What can grandparents who are suddenly parents again do to stretch their money?

For starters, make your money work harder—learn to use it, and learn to stretch it. Tucked away toward the end of the Book of Hebrews is a thought that anyone who handles money should consider: "Keep your lives free from the love of money and be content with what you have" (Hebrews 13:5). The writer does not say it is wrong to be rich or to work hard for money, nor does he say that you are a failure in life if you are poor. He does not say there's something wrong with budgeting carefully and keeping good records to account for the money the Lord gives you. Whether you are rich or poor or somewhere in between, the bottom line is not to let money control you. Instead, you control the money.

The end of verse 5 reminds us of God's promise: "Never will I leave you; never will I forsake you."

In this verse God both reminds us to keep money in its proper perspective and also that He will not leave us nor forsake us. Sort of a you-do-your-part-and-I'll-do-mine exchange. That's why it's important that we get a good handle on finances.

This points us toward working with God to improve our money management skills. Is there a way to make every dollar work harder? If money problems are terrifying you, or if you and your spouse fight about money, is there a way to stop or minimize these fears and disagreements?

The writer of Hebrews adds another thought to that same passage. "The Lord is my helper," he says. "I will not be afraid" (Hebrews 13:6, quoting Psalm 118:6-7). If you are tired of financial tensions, claim God's promise. He helps those who ask for His assistance in learning to manage money. The Lord's idea of assisting you with your money management may involve signing up for a course in bookkeeping at a local school. It may mean reading one or more of Dave Ramsey's excellent books on family money management and following his suggestions. Many churches now offer Ramsey's course "Financial Peace University" to help people increase their money-management skills. The fee to take it is an excellent investment if the knowledge gained can help bring financial peace into your home.

God's bottom line is to keep your life free from the *love* of money or fights with your spouse about money by asking His help in learning to earn money, staying out of debt, and using money responsibly. In other words, learn to be a good steward of what God gives you.

It's not helpful to adopt the attitude of "Oh, I'm not good with numbers. I can't be bothered with any kind of budget. The Lord's eye is on the sparrow—He'll watch over me." If the idea of money management turns you off, remember: you and the sparrow have one thing in common. God gave you all you have. But unlike that sweet little bird, God gave you another ability—to earn and manage the money and other possessions you have. He lets you work to earn it, but ultimately it all belongs to Him. He graciously lets you have the use of what you think of as your own money. He does watch over you, but you are accountable to Him.

The first step is to get as much mileage as possible out of the money you have. This means that it's necessary for you and your spouse—all of the persons who earn and/or spend money in your household—to learn where your money is going. To find out, track your expenses for at least one week, preferably one month. Get a small notebook, and write down your income—every cent you take in from all sources. Also record every cent you spend. Record everything for every day, big and small, weekends and all. A simple listing is all you need.

Start today to track expenses and income. Don't wait for a "usual" month or a time when no special expense is expected. That will never happen. The only thing usual about a month is that you can count on something coming up that will require an expenditure you aren't prepared for—worn-out shoes and clothes, or the automobile insurance premium that's due. Or it's Christmas. Something. Don't try to make an average of several months. Just begin where you are and list every expense and income item for one month.

If you want to keep a record that will be a little easier to sort out at the end of your trial recording period, use a spreadsheet program. Or set up a simple table in your word processing program. Maybe make eight or ten columns with headings like "Food," "Household," "Medical," "Automobile," "Gifts," "Clothing," "Meals Out," "Business." Record every cent you spend. Also put in a column headed "Income." Record in the "Income" column all the money that comes in from all sources.

Keep at it, day after day for at least a week, but keeping track for a month will give you a better overall picture of what's going out. At the end of that time, go through your list and add up all the income lines in one total. Add up all the expense lines in another total. Look carefully through your entries to see where the money went.

If you have never kept an income and expense record before, it could be a real eye-opener. A friend of mine, recording expenses and income for the first time, was amazed to discover what she was spending on shoes and eating out. At the end of her tracking month, she asked herself, "Do I really need all those shoes?" She also asked, "By planning ahead, making a shopping list, and shopping for food at the grocery store once a week could I save time and avoid the extra expense of eating out so often?"

After adding up all that came in and went out for one month, what did you find? Where did the money go? Are you spending more than you make? If so, the very first thing to do is determine areas where you can cut back until you have more coming in than you have going out.

Does your record of expenses show impulse buying of items you don't really need? Another friend of mine, keeping a record of all expenses for the first time, made the startling discovery that the premium coffee she was buying for five dollars a cup every afternoon on the way home from work added an incredible one hundred dollars per month to her expenses.

Look for other possible extravagances. Are you grilling steaks when you should be grilling hamburger? Could you get by with something less than premium cable service? Can you do without the data service on your cell phone? How much cash did you hand over to a teenager who said he was broke and desperate before you remembered that you and he had an agreement that he would earn his own spending money with an after-school job? If you're allowing a teenager to expect you to pick up the difference between what he or she is earning and what he or she is spending, you're doing the teenager no favor.

Let's look at the flip side. Is there a way to increase income? Can you and/or your spouse work a second job? Remember: no job that brings in honest income should be beneath your dignity. It may not be fun, but it can help you increase income.

Based on what you discovered by writing everything down for a month, take your first stab at making a written budget. Give each dollar a place to live. You will make mistakes. The first try will not result in a perfect budget plan. In fact, there may not be any such thing as a perfect budget. But there can be one that is way better than no plan at all.

It's very important that you and your spouse get on the same page and handle money together. If one of you is a saver and the other a spender, perhaps it will be easier for the saver to make a preliminary budget, since that is his or her inclination anyway.

The two of you should then sit down together and work out a compromise. If you're on your own, you'll need to make your own decisions and stick with them.

Decide how you'll structure your budget. It may be easiest to plan a one-month cycle since most billing assumes a one-month sequence. If you get paid every two weeks, perhaps you'll want to set your budget up for two weeks at a time.

The next step is spending your money on paper. Begin with the absolute necessities:

Tithe: give to God, who owns it all anyway and just lets you manage some of it for Him.

Emergency fund/savings: pay yourself.

Food

Shelter: mortgage payment or rent; utilities

Transportation: automobile insurance, car payment, gasoline.

Health: health insurance premium; prescription drugs; co-payments for doctor visits or other medical expenses.

I know a pastor who teaches anyone who asks him about money management the "80-10-10" method. Give away (tithe) ten percent, save (pay yourself) ten percent, and live on 80 percent. I recommend it, even when money is scarce.

What you give to God—your tithe—is a necessary category for serious Christians, as important as food and shelter. People usually consider ten percent as the basic amount for tithe. Generations of God's people have learned what I discovered the hard way. If you give God His share first, He is faithful to stretch the rest to provide what you need.

You may be thinking, *Here I am barely making it, and now you're suggesting I give away ten percent?* I can only tell you what I have proved over and over. I don't pretend to understand God's bookkeeping, but I know there have been times when I have had too little money to meet expenses. From sad experience, I have learned that if I did not pay the tithe, I came up short in the end. *But* if I paid the tithe first, somehow there was enough money to cover everything. I don't understand it; I only know it has proven to be true in my life. I believe that paying the tithe first and watching God stretch the money that's left is known as putting God first in your life, trusting the Lord and finding Him faithful. Remember Hebrews 13:5—"Never will I leave you; never will I forsake you." And God was speaking there in the context of money management.

Second is setting money aside for emergencies. Ideally, in an 80-10-10 plan, this should be another ten percent. If you do not have the funds to save that much, at least establish the category in your budget, setting aside something every payday to build an emergency fund. A killer shoe sale is not an acceptable reason to invade the emergency fund. This fund is for things like unexpected car repairs or a plumbing problem you can't fix yourself. A savings account or a money market account is a good place to keep your emergency fund. It will earn a small amount of interest, and it's available on short notice if something unexpected occurs.

The rest of the list is self-evident. You eat to live, to stay well, to fight another day. A roof over your head is necessary. Transportation comes next. Few of us can walk to work. In some cities, public transportation is available. But in our culture, most of us drive an automobile to work. Some kind of health care is also a necessity.

Armed with the record you have kept of actual expenses for one month, assign a reasonable dollar amount for the tithe and the other five absolute necessities: emergency fund, food, housing, transportation, and health needs.

Do you have money left over? Good! The money you have left over after the necessities of life is called discretionary income. But don't get excited about sudden riches just yet. Instead, give each discretionary dollar a job. Spend all of them on paper. Perhaps this month you need to set aside money for clothes. Or maybe taxes are coming and you need to label that money for the tax bill. Perhaps you can increase the number of dollars allocated to go into the emergency fund savings account. Build the emergency fund until you have at least one thousand dollars set aside for emergencies you hope don't happen. Are you in debt? Pay down debt with these dollars. Begin with the smallest debt and keep whittling away at it until you are free of debt. Know where every dollar goes.

Whatever budget you devise, be prepared for it to not work flawlessly right away. When you are just beginning, it is probably wise to budget a little more in each category than you think you will need. Remain flexible, and don't be too hard on yourself or your spouse. Make adjustments in the different categories for the next month's budget, and try again. It can become a kind of game to get those dollars by the collar and make them behave.

Reassess your budget plan each month—or every two weeks if that is the schedule you decide to use. Sit down again with your spouse and correct the mistakes. Think about what big expenses are coming up and put money aside for them. Keep doing this month after month until you get better at it.

Budgeting tools are available if you feel you need more help. A program called "You Need a Budget" can be downloaded from the Internet for free, but if you continue using it, you'll have to purchase it. You can find it at <www.youneedabudget.com>. Dave Ramsey's books are available in bookstores and on the Internet. They contain valuable "how-to" help in establishing responsible habits in managing money.

Good communication between you and your spouse, if you have one, is important. You make up the "budget committee" at your house. Sit down together each month to decide on any needed budget changes and/or special needs for the coming month. If an emergency arises, or if there is a change of any kind in the financial outlook, discuss it together immediately. In fact, discussions about money and its uses must be an ongoing topic of conversation in a successful marriage. If one or the other of you is uncomfortable with how you are handling money, it should be brought up and openly discussed. Don't discuss it when either of you is angry, but choose a time when you are both calm and be ready to explain what is bothering you. Come to a compromise or a better understanding of the family's money policies. Never lie about money or withhold financial information from your spouse.

People who are raising kids who are not their own usually need all the financial help they can get. Most states have some kind of taxpayer help for grandparents or other relatives who are raising grandchildren or other children that are not their own. Before investigating whether you are eligible for any benefits programs, it is essential to get your personal finances in order and a budget in place. Once you have your financial house in order with accurate figures available to give to an agency that may ask, then by all means find and apply for any public monies for which you may be eligible. When applying for public benefits, almost certainly you will be asked about your income and expenses. If you have your budget figures readily available, it will facilitate matters a great deal. Be prepared to make your case honestly but vigorously.

States vary. The place to start to find out whether you are eligible for taxpayer-funded financial help is probably whatever state agency is responsible for seeing that children are not abused or neglected. As mentioned previously, in some states this is called the Department of Social Services. It may be called the Cabinet for Family Services or something similar to one of these in your state. Your local Area Agency on Aging may also be able to point you in the right direction. If you have relative children—that is, children with whom you have some tie of blood or family—who were removed from their birth parents and placed with you because of abuse or neglect, the social worker or other employee with whom you dealt at the time of the placement should be able to supply you with names and phone numbers of persons who can help you find any financial help that is available and for which you may be eligible. The American Association of Retired Persons has available on its web site, < www.aarp.org>, a Benefits QuickLINK Questionnaire for each state. It's intended to help you determine your potential eligibility for benefits programs.

How much public money you may be entitled to is influenced by, among other factors, your legal relationship to the children. It's possible to become a foster parent to children to whom you have a blood-kin relationship. In that case, you'll be paid whatever your state pays foster parents. However, when you are a foster parent only, the state maintains custody of the children, even if you are the kids' biological grandparents. This means that the responsible officials can decide to remove the children from your care because you are functioning as a foster parent and not as a relative caregiver. On the other hand, if you have legal custody of the children, you can make decisions for them and they cannot be removed from your care without a court hearing. The amount of assistance to which you are entitled may be less than if you were a foster parent only. In some states, if a court appoints you legal guardian of your grandchildren or other relative children, you may be eligible for what is called a subsidized guardianship program. California, for example, calls their subsidized guardianship program "kin-GAP" (Guardianship Assistance Program).

If you adopt the children, in the eyes of the law they are as much yours as if they had been born to you. You will not be eligible for any public support that other persons who have a less binding form of relationship may qualify for. You may, however, still be eligible for Medicaid or other public subsidy. Each state is different. Usually some financial assistance is available if you have primary parental responsibility for children not your own.

Remember: God owns everything we have. We all hold our possessions in trust for Him. This certainly does not mean you have no responsibility to take care of your money. If you don't know why you are perpetually broke and can never seem to get ahead financially, try the simple recordkeeping outlined in this chapter. You will be surprised to learn what those slippery dollars have been doing while your back was turned. If it is God's money, He will surely confirm His promise to stay with you and be your helper. Trust God, put Him first, and watch Him work with you toward a financially secure life.

**God expects you to be a good steward
of what He has entrusted to you.**

*Lord, help me as I learn to manage well
all you have provided.*

Questions for Support Group Discussion

1. Discuss what the Bible says about being either rich or poor.

2. Discuss the 80-10-10 method of managing money.

3. Has anyone in the group kept a record of what he or she has coming in each month as well as what is going out?

4. Discuss the benefits of keeping such a record as you formulate a budget.

5. Discuss the promises in the Bible about God's care of those who put Him first.

eleven

RECOGNIZING THE SIGNS OF SUBSTANCE ABUSE

"I'll never forget that cold, snowy night," Richard said. "The police called us about midnight to say they had raided Greg and Rachel's house. They found drug paraphernalia and other evidence. They were removing the children from their parents' custody, charging abuse and neglect plus drug use. As always, the officials were looking for relatives who would take the children rather than sending them to foster care with strangers. They asked if we would take the kids. Put up or shut up, or they'll go to foster homes with strangers tonight.

"We went and got them. What else could we do? Jordan was four then, and Jill was just one year old."

"If only we had known sooner," Richard said. "I suspected something was going on with Greg, our oldest son. But my wife, Shirley, and I rationalized that he was just a kid and would be fine. But he wasn't. We were too ignorant to recognize the signs."

You may remember Richard and Shirley from an earlier chapter. They have three grown children, are committed Christians, and taught their children about Jesus from infancy. They were, and still are, active in a Bible-believing church. They're both in their fifties and both college graduates. Richard writes and edits in the public relations department of a major corporation. Shirley left a career in banking to be a stay-at-home mom when their own kids were young. She had gone back into a job in the financial industry when she had to quit to care for their son's children. Richard and Shirley learned the hard way that no home is immune to drug abuse, even homes where Christian values are central in their parenting.

Home-schooled, as were his younger siblings, Greg switched to a public school for his junior year of high school with his parents' blessing. An excellent athlete, a local high school recruited him to play baseball. He was seventeen.

Almost immediately his parents noticed changes. "It was a job to push him through his junior year," recalls Richard. "That big change in his attitude toward school should have been a red flag. But we missed it. In his senior year, I dropped him off at school each morning. We found out later that he walked through the building, out the back door, and never attended school that year at all. Greg agreed to see a counselor, who diagnosed extreme depression. The counselor did not mention that depression could be a symptom of marijuana use. There are other reasons for depression, but I wish we had known enough to at least consider that the depression could have been from drug abuse."

The use of drugs was becoming more prevalent when Richard and Shirley were teens, but small-town, middle-class America wasn't taking drug use seriously yet. Richard remembers that when he was growing up in a small Midwestern town, there was one drug addict in town he knew of. Richard never knew his name. The man, a talented architect, lost his job in a nearby city because he became addicted to morphine, the only drug of abuse readily available in that time and place. He eked out a living as a handyman in the local hardware store. Richard remembers hearing his elders refer to him as a "dope fiend" with a combination of laughter and disgust at seeing a well-educated, highly intelligent man waste his life. He learned as a youngster to equate drug abuse with stupidity, nothing any sensible person would touch. When their son's habits and attitudes changed abruptly, his parents did not even consider the possibility that Greg was abusing drugs.

When he was eighteen, Greg got a job at a fast-food restaurant and left home to share an apartment with another young man. Although Richard and Shirley were disappointed that Greg had no interest in going to college, they were more distressed when they learned he had quit attending church. They had reared their children in church, doing their best to live out a Christian lifestyle. But they accepted Greg as he was, keeping in touch, grateful that he had a job and was self-supporting. When Greg was about twenty, he met Rachel. They never married but have been together for several years and have two children.

"We love Rachel like a daughter," says Richard, "but we didn't plan on having to raise their kids."

Greg and Rachel were using—and still use—alcohol, methamphetamine, and marijuana. Officials ultimately terminated Greg's and Rachel's parental rights, another way of saying the authorities did not think the two of them would ever be able to parent their children.

"I'm a fish-or-cut-bait kind of guy," Richard said. "When social services terminated Greg and Rachel's parental rights and the kids were freed for adoption, I said to Shirley that we should just adopt them. They were living with us anyway. I knew that if we adopted, they would be ours, no questions asked. It would limit what their natural parents could do and get the government agencies off our backs. But I'll tell you one thing—I'm learning what to look for if I'm ever suspicious that my grandkids are using drugs. We won't let things get out of hand again."

Since that time, doctors have diagnosed little Jill with fetal alcohol syndrome, which has resulted in mental, physical, and behavioral problems.

What are the signs of drug abuse?

Giving age-appropriate information about drug use to children is like teaching the Ten Commandments. It's never too early to begin. Let toddlers come to consciousness knowing that theirs is a drug-free family and that abusing drugs is wrong. Don't underestimate the age at which children can be enticed into drug use. A 2005 study found that sixteen and a half percent of eighth-graders admitted to having used marijuana at some time. The number was 44.8 percent for twelfth-graders. That's almost half. Don't wait. Have talks early and often about abusing drugs.[1]

But suppose, in spite of your best efforts, you suspect your grandchildren are using. What should you look for? How can you confirm it?

One obvious and often overlooked way to find out what's going on is to ask. Don't do it when either you or the child is angry. Don't hitch it to another topic. Wait until a time when you can talk quietly, one-on-one, shedding more light and less heat on the subject. Don't make accusations, and ask in a non-threatening way. Let the child know you love him or her, want the best for him or her. You're not trying to put the child down. You're inquiring for information. The child may deny using drugs, even if he or she is, so be prepared for that. It's important that you know the signs of drug use, and mention the child's behaviors that led you to wonder. Pray hard for guidance before that conversation and for wisdom in confronting and dealing with it if it becomes apparent that there is a problem.

What Richard and Shirley observed in Greg were clues—major changes in behavior, new attitudes toward school, and new friends. True, changes can occur for reasons other than drug use, so look also for depression, withdrawal, and hostility. Has the child become careless about grooming? Is he or she having trouble getting along with friends? Does he or she suddenly have a lot of new friends? Is he or she taking part in sports or other activities as usual, or has he or she lost interest in activities? Does the child ignore curfews? Does the child sometimes disappear for hours with no good explanation of where he or she was or what he or she was doing?

The following are some things to watch for in each of the major groups of commonly abused drugs.

Cannabinoids

Also called marijuana or hashish, signs may include

- Red, bloodshot eyes
- Unsteadiness on his or her feet
- Difficulty remembering things
- Silly behavior for no reason

Richard says he wishes now that he had followed the advice he credits to television comedian Bill Cosby: Don't be shy. When the kid is gone, go into his or her room and sniff around. Are there any unusual odors on his or her clothes or in his or her room? Look under the mattress. Be a snoop. If you find drug paraphernalia—drug pipes, rolling papers—almost certainly smoking marijuana and perhaps other illegal substances are not far away. Does he or she use a lot of room deodorizers? Don't forget that drug paraphernalia may include such items as a felt-tip marker with a concealed drug pipe, a lipstick dispenser hiding a drug pipe, soda cans with false bottoms, or a fake pager to conceal illegal drugs.[2]

Drug paraphernalia is sometimes made in bright, fashionable colors to attract teenagers. It's illegal to sell or offer such gear for sale. While it may be sold in "head shops" or trendy novelty shops, don't forget that gas stations and convenience stores sometimes sell illegal drug paraphernalia.[3]

Depressants

Depressants include anti-anxiety drugs and tranquilizers. Many of them are legal prescription drugs and have names we've heard: Phenobarbital, Librium, Valium, Xanax, Ativan, and Klonopin, among others.

Depressant drugs may be prescribed legally by a doctor to calm nerves and relax muscles. But when someone is taking large doses or improperly using these drugs, you may observe

- Confusion
- Lack of coordination; shaking
- Inability to concentrate
- Falling asleep at work or school or other inappropriate times

Be sure children under your care understand that depressant drugs used with alcohol can stop breathing and cause death.[4]

Club Drugs

Club drugs include MDMA (ecstasy), Rohypnol (flunitrazepam), GHB (gamma-hydroxybutyrate), and ketamine, a dissociative anesthetic. They are called "club drugs" because some teens and young adults who are attracted to the so-called nightclub, bar, rave, or trance scene use them to produce intoxicating highs. These drugs are said to be inexpensive, another reason for their popularity. Raves and trances are usually all-night dances, often held in warehouses.

In addition to usual depressant symptoms, these drugs can produce permanent brain damage and other devastating effects that may not be immediately apparent, even to the most watchful parent. Two of the club drugs are also called "date-rape drugs." These are Rohypnol and GHP. Often colorless, tasteless, and odorless, they can be added to beverages and consumed unknowingly. Rohypnol incapacitates its victims, preventing them from resisting sexual assault. It may also rob one of memory while under its influence. This is the reason anyone, but especially young women, should never leave any drink—even a glass of water—unattended.

MDMA, or ecstasy, is a stimulant. It appears to cause permanent brain damage.[5] MDMA in high doses can interfere with the body's ability to regulate temperature. On rare but unpredictable occasions, this can lead to a sharp increase in body temperature, organ failure, and death.[6]

Dissociative Anesthetics

Ketamine and PCP, the chief drugs in the class of dissociative anesthetics, were developed originally as general anesthetics for surgery. They are called "dissociative anesthetics" because they "distort perceptions of sight and sound and produce feelings of detachment—dissociation from" the user's surroundings and self.[7]

Things to watch for if you suspect someone is using a dissociative drug include

• Increased heart rate and blood pressure
• Impaired motor function
• Memory loss.

High doses of Ketamine produce delirium, depression, even cause depressed lung function and arrest. In other words, it may cause you to stop breathing. PCP may decrease blood pressure and heart rate. PCP can produce panic, aggression, violence, and loss of appetite as well as depression. These symptoms of use are all easily observed.

Hallucinogens

LSD (lysergic acid diethylamide), mescaline, and psilocybin are hallucinogens. Hallucinogens have been used for thousands of years to induce states of detachment from reality. Cultural leaders have used them in social and religious rituals to produce mystical visions. LSD was originally derived from a rye fungus by the German chemist Albert Hofmann. It is now produced synthetically. Use of hallucinogens has increased greatly since the 1960s. LSD has no accepted medical use in the United States. It has been called "the most potent mood- and perception-altering drug known"[8] and may produce mental disorders.

LSD and mescaline may cause
- Increased body temperature, heart rate, and blood pressure
- Loss of appetite
- Sleeplessness
- Numbness, weakness, tremors

Opioids and Morphine Derivatives

Codeine, fentanyl, heroin, morphine, opium, oxycodone HCL, and hydrocodone bitartrate are among the drugs in the group of opioids and morphine derivatives. Many of the pain relievers commonly taken without damage can be used illegally. Robitussin A-C and Tylenol No. 3 both contain codeine and are legally used only by prescription. When overused, many of the effects can be easily observed. These may include

- Euphoria—an exaggerated or unaccountable elation—or drowsiness
- Nausea, constipation, and confusion (may also accompany use of opium derivatives)

While many opium derivatives are legal for use as pain relievers or anesthetics, it should be understood that these drugs are capable of producing breathing problems, unconsciousness, and death.

Stimulants

Look for injecting or inhaling paraphernalia. Methamphetamine, cocaine, the club drug MDMA (also called ecstasy) and other stimulant drugs can cause

- Nervousness
- Anorexia and weight loss
- Inability to sleep

Methamphetamine and cocaine can cause

- Impaired memory
- Aggressiveness

- Psychotic behavior, as well as damage to the heart and nervous system

MDMA is toxic to the heart and liver and can cause kidney failure.[9]

Cocaine and methamphetamine are the best known in the group. Nicotine, the active ingredient in tobacco, is a stimulant. Tobacco smoking, of course, is the usual means for taking nicotine. Introducing either tobacco or marijuana smoke into lungs appears to promote lung cancer and chronic lung disease. In addition, nicotine produces bad pregnancy outcomes, cardiovascular disease, stroke, and addiction.[10] As with other drugs, notice any unidentified odors clinging to your child's clothing or lingering in his or her room at home.

Anabolic Steroids

Use of steroids has increased markedly in young persons as reports of its widespread use by professional sport stars have become known. Steroids have no intoxicating effects; however, they create observable signs of use. They may produce

- High blood pressure
- Blood clotting and cholesterol changes
- Kidney or liver cancer
- Hostility, aggression
- Acne, although there are other causes for acne
- In adolescents, premature stoppage of growth
- In males, prostate cancer, reduced sperm production, shrunken testicles, breast enlargement
- In females, menstrual irregularities, development of a beard and other masculine characteristics

Inhalants

Adults attempting to steer young persons away from abusing drugs need to realize that common household products such as spray paint, hairspray, nail polish, and anything else in an aerosol container can be "huffed," "sniffed," or "bagged" for a quick, inexpensive high.

Things to watch for include
- Hidden rags or empty containers of products that may be abused
- Chemical odor on the user's breath or clothing
- Paint stains on his or her face, hands, or clothing
- Appearance of drunkenness with slurred or incoherent speech and lack of coordination

Huffing is soaking a rag or a piece of clothing in an inhalant and pressing the cloth to your mouth. Sniffing is sniffing or snorting fumes from an aerosol container into your nose or mouth. Bagging is done by spraying or pouring a product into a plastic or paper bag and inhaling the fumes.

Huffing, sniffing, or bagging can cause choking or seizures. If the inhalants displace oxygen within the lungs or block air from entering the lungs, death by asphyxiation or suffocation can follow.[11]

Richard and Shirley, who are raising their son's two children, wanted to learn the signs of illegal use of drugs to avoid repeating with their grandchildren the mistakes of ignorance they made when their son began to use drugs. Richard says with the wisdom of hindsight that part of the problem is right at home. "It's your house. Make kids accountable while they are in your home. Don't trust them too much. Don't give them so much rope that they wind up hanging themselves. Just be informed. Read the things your kids are writing. Listen to the kids talking."

If you suspect your child is using drugs, other things to watch for in addition to those already mentioned include
- Increase in borrowing money
- New use of breath mints or mouthwash to cover the smell of alcohol

- New use of eye drops to mask bloodshot eyes or dilated pupils
- Changes in sleeping patterns
- Significant mood changes
- Hostility, lack of cooperation
- Furtive or secretive behavior, locked doors
- Emotional instability
- Loss of interest in or changes in personal appearance
- Hyperactive or hyper-aggressive behavior
- Declining grades[12]

"You may have one child that you suspect is up to something. Don't let your spouse convince you that everything is fine because they are just kids," says Richard. "As a husband and wife team, set clear, defined boundaries and stick to them. You can't give in. You can't enable kids to keep on. Greg is twenty-six now and a heartbreak to us. In spite of plenty of opportunity to get help, he makes no effort to break his addictions." Richard continues: "His sister Janet is twenty-three, a college graduate, married to a good guy. She is puzzled by her older brother's way of life and wonders if Greg has gone crazy. Our youngest, Bruce, is seventeen and still at home. He seems to enjoy his new little brother and sister and is a big help with them."

"Why is Greg so different from the others?" I asked.

Richard laughs bitterly. "Martha, if you find the answer to that, let me know, would you?" He reports that until about a year and a half ago, Greg was able to function well enough to hold a job. Now the years of addiction have taken their toll. He and Rachel are barely functional, mostly living in their car because neither can hold a steady job.

"This is all so different," says Richard. "It's been an education. Everywhere I go I run into people raising their grandchildren. Or I talk with someone who says he or she has a friend, a brother, or a sister—someone—who is in the same boat.

"We serve a God who forgave us," Richard adds, "so we forgive Greg. But I wish we had known what to look for sooner. Maybe things would have turned out differently."

**Arm yourself with knowledge to help you
recognize potential pitfalls.**

*Father, open my eyes and give me wisdom to
recognize signs of substance abuse.*

Questions for Support Group Discussion

1. Discuss the various drugs and types of drugs mentioned in this chapter. Do any of the grandparents in the group know or suspect that a child in their care is using drugs?

2. Discuss behaviors to watch for in children and teens that will alert you to children's possible drug use.

3. Is there anything grandparents can do to "drug-proof" their grandchildren? What are some ways grandparents can help their grandchildren realize the dangers of drug use?

4. Encourage grandparents who are raising their grandchildren because of their adult children's drug use to talk about the toll it has taken on their family.

twelve

WHERE IS HOPE?

Psalm 116:1-2 says, "I love the LORD, for he heard my voice. . . . I will call on him as long as I live."

Vickie is a grandmother raising her heroin-addicted daughter's two toddlers. I asked her what the two or three biggest concerns in her life are, now that she's a parent again.

"Money comes first," she said. "Children are expensive. Next I suppose is my legal relationship to the kids. I'm always scared my daughter will show up out of the blue and try to get them back. If I adopt them, she can't ever get them back, but my 'kin-care' money from the state will stop. And I need the money."

Vickie paused and looked at me. Her eyes were sad and tired. "You know what's really at the top? I feel alone. Nobody cares about me and these precious babies. What on earth would happen to them if I died? I'm sixty-two years old. I try not to think about it."

The words of Psalm 116 went through my mind: "The cords of death entangled me, the anguish of the grave came upon me" (Psalm 116:3). Grandmother Vickie works all day, picks the kids up from daycare, and prepares their supper. After they eat and she cleans up, she is exhausted. All she feels like doing is sitting. But it's the kids' only opportunity for play time with her, and they're ready for a romp. Somehow she finds the energy to play with them briefly before the bedtime routine begins. The next day she does it all over again.

"I have to take it one day at a time," she says. Somehow she puts one foot in front of the other, plodding through the days. She's getting older, she's tired, and she doesn't have enough money. But determined and plucky, she keeps going for the sake of the much-loved grandbabies whose parents, for whatever reason, cannot raise their own children.

Vickie's plight is an increasingly common cultural shift in the United States. The middle generation has fallen out, and grandparents, alarmed at the thought of their grandchildren going into the state's foster care system to be parented by strangers, take full parental responsibility to raise their grandchildren.

Is there hope? Are there words of comfort for overworked, over-stressed grandparents?

Psalm 116 is strikingly personal from beginning to end. It describes the human condition without pulling any punches and tells of God's loving response to those who cry to Him for help.

In fact, the first thing the psalmist tells us in verse 1 is God's response to his cry for help was that God heard his prayer. That is an excellent reason for gratitude to the Lord and making a daily habit of prayer.

The psalmist was doing what every Christian knows should be done first: pray. Nothing takes the place of turning everything over to the Lord and remembering that the Lord hears and answers prayer. If that sounds like a cliché, it is, because the truth of it does not change. Another cliché is that prayer changes things. It, too, came to my mind because, like many clichés, it's true. Prayer *does* make a difference. God *does* hear and answer.

The writer of this psalm understood that humans tend to panic sometimes. We are certain our troubles will drown us. The psalmist knew that when we are drowning in responsibilities beyond our strength to carry them, the thing to do is pray. If you are a grandparent raising grandchildren, your situation fits that pattern.

How and for what should you pray?

First of all, the Lord prefers honest prayers. Tell Him that you feel too tired and have too much work to do. That's not whining; that's just telling it like it is. If you're angry with your irresponsible child who has gotten into drugs and can't raise his or her own babies, tell the Lord that too. He already knows how you feel, but it does you good to get it off your chest by telling Him. It is especially good to be able to tell it to He who loves you and has your best interest at heart. That is our God. One of the miracles of serving such a big God is that He can listen to millions of prayers all at once from all over His world and He can give each one of those praying persons His full, undivided attention. I don't know how He does that; I just know it happens. It is another one of those God-things, like His ability to stretch money.

Pray for yourself. What do you need? What bugs you?

Pray for your grandchild the things you would pray for any child dear to you. Pray that he or she will find Jesus as Savior and make Him Lord of his or her life. Pray that he or she will do his or her very best in school. Pray that he or she will be kept from physical harm, including drug addiction.

Pray for your grandchild's wrong-headed parents, your child and his or her partner or spouse. Pray they will find their way to God. Perhaps they may even be able to parent their own child some day.

Pray for your own peace. Pray for physical and emotional strength. Pray for wisdom in discerning the difference between helping and enabling your child—your grandchild's parent.

Pray about anything that is on your heart or mind. Sometimes you hear jokes about praying for parking places as though that were too simpleminded for God to bother with. It's not. The underlying principle is sound. God loves us as individuals. He is interested in the details of our lives. He will not turn you away if you come to Him with the smallest request—the day's quietest need. We are His little children. He will not turn us away any more than we would turn away a little child clinging to us. It may be little to Him—everything is little to God—but if it is fearsome to us, like any good parent, He takes it seriously, listening to our prayer.

Psalm 116:5-6 lists some of God's traits of character. He is gracious, righteous, merciful. Our great God is adequate in all situations. That is not the same as saying our lives will always be easy.

In Psalm 116:7 the psalmist counsels with himself. He talks to his own soul. "Rest, my soul," he says. *Why?* God has been good to you. In the middle of all his troubles, he has to admit that God has done a lot of good things for him. It's difficult to remember and be grateful for the good when you are in the middle of the bad. It's much easier to concentrate on the bad that is looming big before you. But the psalmist persists in finding good in his situation. He doggedly lists God's blessings. He has been delivered from spiritual death, sorrow, and wrong decisions—"death . . . tears . . . stumbling" in verses 8 and 9. According to verse 9, the reason the Lord delivered him from all these bad things was to free him up to be able to walk with the Lord. How wonderful to realize that the Creator of the entire universe wants you to walk with Him—He enjoys your company!

In spite of his troubles, the psalmist is so carried away with God's kindness that he is looking for ways to repay God for His goodness (verse 12). This is real progress. In verse 1 he is in anguish, crying for mercy. By verse 12 he is so grateful for all the good things God has done for him that he vows he will obey the Lord no matter what. He will even express such a vow publicly, "in the presence of all his [God's] people" (verse 14). It sounds as if he means to tell some of his fellow church members how God is dealing with him.

The writer then comes upon a truth we all need to remember: We are precious to the Lord, so dear that He observes the death of each of His people (v. 15). Christians do not die alone. If we know Him as Savior, God is there for us in the hour of death.

He comes finally to the height of his thought. He has moved beyond self-pity. He has faced his problems with God's help. Even though life may still be hard, he will do what he has promised God. He will obey God's will for his life insofar as he knows it. And even though things are not perfect and life is still difficult, he will praise God.

The psalmist describes the sacrifice of praise—praising God when you don't feel like it (verse 17). The sacrifice of praise can be one of the hardest yet one of the most helpful things we can do. Even in sorrow and trouble, when it is not easy but rather a real sacrifice to do so, I will praise God. The sacrifice of praise is a real gift to God. The psalmist closes his psalm by saying he will live for the Lord and do all of these things in public, in the midst of his church family. He vows to not be a secret believer. He is going to tell others out loud in public how good God is to him.

How can the grandparent raising grandchildren apply this teaching to his or her situation?

Doing what Psalm 116 outlines is an excellent start toward emotional well-being when faced with huge problems. First the psalmist cries to God for help. Then he looks for the good things in life and acknowledges God's role in them. He follows this by thanking God even when he does not feel like it, offering the sacrifice of thanksgiving.

Psalm 116 does not say so, but the path of action the psalmist outlines is one of the best remedies for depression. Thinking positively about the good things in your life—and we all have some good things—is an excellent way to overcome depression.

Grandparents who are parenting their own grandchildren must resolve in their minds and hearts that this whole thing is not totally their fault. *My child may be wasting his or her life and unable to parent his or her own children, but it does not automatically mean that I was a failure as a parent.* You can expect sadness and a sense of failure when you first realize that your child cannot raise his or her own kids, but it does not have to be a settled frame of mind. Of course, you were not a perfect parent; nobody is. But because your parenting was not always perfect does not lead to the conclusion that you must assume blame for your child's wrong choices. Your child was old enough to know better when he or she made the decisions that left him or her unable to parent his or her own child.

You may have issues you need to resolve—anger, guilt, bitterness, regret, sadness, grief. These emotions are not abnormal responses to the news that you are going to be parenting again. It does not show a lack of faith in the Lord's ability to deliver you from a burden of anger, guilt, or sadness if you get professional help with these problems.

God very often uses other human beings to bring about emotional and physical healing. The healing and solutions to problems that appear in answer to prayer and praise are no less God's work in our lives if friends or professionals help us than if God had healed us with a thunderclap. Perhaps God will use someone in your church family to help you bear the burden. Perhaps a professional Christian counselor can guide you to acceptance of your new and unexpected role as a grandparent becoming a parent again. The Lord uses others to help us, just as He frequently uses trips to the doctor and medicines from the drug store to heal us physically. The healing, either emotional or physical, comes from the God who loves us unconditionally. God does not love us any less, nor is He ultimately any less responsible for the healing because He uses other people in the process of restoring us.

As you become accustomed to having a child in your household again and see your grandchild settling in, let it remind you of your relationship with Jesus Christ. The little child bonding and attaching to an adult who loves him or her, is always there, and has his or her best interest at heart becomes a parable of the Christian life.

We've talked about how children need to attach to a trusted adult in order to develop normal adult relationships. Those who commit themselves to God discover this principle early on. As we get to know God revealed in Christ Jesus, we find Him faithful in every area. He is there for us, just as you, a trusted adult, are there for your grandchild. Christianity is not a religion so much as it is a love relationship with God. As we obey God's known will for us, growing in Him, God in Christ convinces the believer that He does love unconditionally and that His discipline is for our own good. That's how we hope our grandchildren will see us as they get to know us better. We hope they see that we love them un-conditionally and are disciplining only for their own good, never because we are angry.

The best solution to life's trials for humanity, usually realized after some calamities of our own making, is understanding the benefits of putting God first in our lives. Like the little child who is emotionally attached to a parent or other loving caregiver, the child of God who is firmly attached to God the Father obeys God's will for his or her life because he or she loves Him and has grown to trust Him unreservedly. We obey people we trust.

Beyond a doubt, grandparents who find themselves raising their children's children are in a difficult position. At a time in life when you expected you would be doing fun things with your grandchildren, you must take total parental responsibility for ev-erything from midnight feedings and diapers for tiny children to enforcing boundaries and consequences on older children. You have been there and done that! You still love your wayward child, and you love that child's children—your grandchildren. But you are twenty or thirty years older than when you did all of this the first time.

Although it is difficult, you are more than willing to do it to give your precious grandchildren a family and a heritage, a sense of place and stability that being moved from place to place in the foster care system cannot provide.

At some point you will probably get to the point of not caring anymore what your child thinks of your decisions. He or she has failed to carry his or her responsibilities. You cannot be influenced in your decisions by the effect they will have on your child. Grandparents overwhelmed by caring for the grandchildren, and feeling guilt and pain and agonizing because of their child's failure, should ask themselves, *Who is working hardest here?*

Parent Counselor Gene Doyle says that the answer is that if you are spending more time and effort to solve your child's problems than your child is, then you are rescuing and enabling. You need to back off and get on with the business of raising the grandchildren without worrying about what your child thinks.

The bottom line is that God responds to our requests and our praises in prayer. With God's help, either with or without help from human professionals, we can work through blaming ourselves for our child's failure. We can get victory over the anger at undependable children who have left us to raise our grandchildren.

Are there any happy stories of grandparents raising grandchildren? Indeed, there are many, even when they are tinged with tragedy. Not all cases of grandparents raising grandchildren are rooted in drugs and alcohol.

One summer afternoon Cynthia and her husband were entertaining guests on the patio of their home. She pointed to a little girl playing with other children in her neighbor's yard.

"Dr. Cary, do you recognize that child?" she asked one of her guests.

"I can't say that I do. Should I? Who is she?"

"Do you remember the day about ten years ago that you delivered a baby from a young mother injured in an automobile crash who was being kept on life support until her baby could be born? You were working in the emergency room at St. Joseph hospital then."

"I do remember that," said the doctor. "I've wondered sometimes what became of that child."

"There she is—a happy, well-adjusted fifth-grader!" said Cynthia. "They gave her the name her parents had already picked out: Brianna."

Brianna's mother, eight and a half months pregnant, had headed for what she thought would be her last doctor's appointment before her first child was born. It was, but not as she had imagined. As she pulled out of her driveway, an oncoming truck slammed into her vehicle. She was fatally injured. Prompt action by emergency medical personnel kept her on life support until the baby could be delivered, alive and healthy. Then the young mother died.

The devastated twenty-something father turned to his parents. They turned to the mother's parents. The two sets of grandparents, not well acquainted then, looked at each other and said, "With God's help we can do this." And they did.

The mother's parents took the newborn into their home. The baby's father and his parents stayed in close touch, assisting and loving. Five years went by. The young man married again, and his first daughter joined that new household. But the first years in her grandparents' home were a firm, irreplaceable foundation for her life.

"Grandfamilies" are increasing. Without them, a significant number of young people would be lost emotionally and perhaps even physically. Brave grandparents are making a difference—including you. God bless you.

God hears and answers your prayers.

Lord, thank you for loving me and
hearing me when I call on you.

Questions for Support Group Discussion

1. Encourage grandparents to talk about their three or four most urgent concerns as they raise their grandchildren.

2. Discuss the range of emotions grandparents experienced when they realized they would be raising another family.

3. Discuss ways grandparents have coped with the changes to their plans for their lives.

4. Ask grandparents to share what they consider to be the best part of parenting again.

NOTES

Chapter 1

1. <www.census.gov/Press-Release/www/releases/archives/facts_for _features_special_editions/>, AARP Foundation, "State Fact Sheets for Grandparents and Other Relatives Raising Children," <http://www.grand factsheets.org/state_fact_sheets.cfm>. Unless otherwise noted, all statistics in this chapter are from the grandfactsheets web site.

2. JoAnn Wise, (Judge, Fayette County, Kentucky, Circuit Court, Family Court), interview with the author, October 10, 2007, at Lexington, Kentucky, Public Library, Beaumont Branch.

3. <www.census.gov/Press-Release/www/releases/archives/facts_for _features_special_editions/>, Timothy N. Philpot, (Judge, Fayette County, Kentucky, Circuit Court, Family Court), interview with the author, November 26, 2007, in the judge's chambers, Lexington, Kentucky.

4. Rachel Cochran, (Social Services Worker, Cabinet for Health and Family Services, Division of Protection and Permanency, Kentucky), interview with the author by telephone, December 5, 2007.

5. David Godfrey, *A Handbook for Kentucky Grandparents and Other Relative Caregivers.* (Lexington, Ky.: Access to Justice Foundation Legal HelpLine for Older Kentuckians, 2007), 38.

6. Legal Aid Network of Kentucky, "General Information About Paternity," Page now discontinued.

Chapter 2

1. Separated Parenting Access & Resource Center, "Different Types of Child Custody," <http://www.deltabravo.net/custody/typesofcustody.php>.

2. Godfrey, *A Handbook for Kentucky Grandparents*, 1.

3. Richard Woolums (agent, Nicholasville, Kentucky, State Farm Insurance Companies), in an interview by telephone with the author, January 22, 2008.

4. Godfrey, *A Handbook for Kentucky Grandparents,* 57.

5. Saul Spigel, "Grandparents' Custody of Granchildren," 2003-R-0596, OLR Research Report, <http://www.cga.ct.gov/2003/olrdata/kid/ rpt/2003-R-0596.htm>.

6. Carl D. Devine, J. D., (partner, Miller, Griffin & Marks, Lexington, Kentucky), in an interview with the author at the office of the University of Kentucky Cooperative Extension Service, August 20, 2007.

7. This list is derived from Kentucky Revised Statutes 403.270.

8. Godfrey, *A Handbook for Kentucky Grandparents*, 15-18; Judge JoAnn Wise, interview with the author, October 10, 2007, at Lexington (Ky.) Public Library, Beaumont Branch.

9. Godfrey, *A Handbook for Kentucky Grandparents*, 2, 5-8.

Chapter 3

1. <http://www.pueblo.gsa.gov/cic>.

2. Carl D. Devine, interview with the author August 20, 2007. Mr. Devine also gave other valuable information used in this chapter.

3. AARP, "Help for Grandparents Raising Grandchildren. Formal Kinship Care," <http://www.aarp.org/relationships/grandparenting>; Judge JoAnn Wise, interview with the author, October 10, 2007, at Lexington (Ky.), Public Library, Beaumont Branch. Judge Wise also gave other valuable information used in this chapter.

4. Information given from Sharon Olson, V.P., Grandfamilies of America, in a personal communication to the author. on the Kinship Caregiver Support Act is derived from materials made available by the Child Welfare and Mental Health Division of the Children's Defense Fund. For more information, the division may be reached at their web site, <http://www.childrensdefense.org>, or at 202-662-3568.

Chapter 4

1. Kentucky Cabinet for Health & Family Services—Adoption Glossary, 1.

2. For an excellent discussion of RAD and therapeutic parenting methods, see Nancy L. Thomas, *When Love Is Not Enough: A Guide to Parenting Children with RAD—Reactive Attachment Disorder* (Glenwood Spring, Colo.: Families by Design, 1997).

3. See <www.aacap.org>, <http://www.answers.com>.

4. Otto Kaak (University of Kentucky faculty member, psychiatrist), speaking at the 8th Annual Bluegrass Region Grandparents and relatives As Parents (GAP) conference, Lexington, Kentucky, March 20, 2008.

5. Thomas, *When Love Is Not Enough*, 101.

6. <www.answers.com/topic/attachment-disorder>.

7. Kaak, GAP conference, March 20, 2008.

8. Thomas, *When Love Is Not Enough*, 67; see also 18-19, 28, 33, 53; <www.answers.com/topic/attachment-disorder>.

9. For parenting methods for use with unattached children and an excellent discussion on this and other parenting problems, see Gregory C.

Keck and Regina M. Kupecky, *Parenting the Hurt Child: Helping Adoptive Families Heal and Grow* (Colorado Springs: Piñon Press, 2002). See pages 67-68 for why this point is true.

10. Kentucky Cabinet for Health & Family Services—Adoption Glossary, 5.

11. <www.emedicine.com/ped/topic2646.htm>. Patricia Metcalf Johnson (adoptive parent and education specialist), interview with the author at Wilmore Senior Community Center at Wesley Village, June 19, 2008.

12. Preschool Attendance Grows Under Government's Hand," *In Brief,* Foundation for Economic Education, e-mail newsletter, May 12, 2008.

13. <www.answers.com/topic/attachment-disorder>.

14. Thomas, 100-101.

15. Kaak, GAP conference, March 20, 2008.

16. <www.answers.com/topic/attachment-disorder>.

17. Thomas, *When Love Is Not Enough*, 43-47.

Chapter 5

1. American Academy of Pediatrics at <http://www.aap.org/publiced/BR_ADHD.htm>.

2. "ADHD & Your Child: Making a Plan," Healthy Advice Networks, 2007, 7. Free educational brochure published with the sponsorship of Mc-Neil-PPC, makers of Concerta, one of many drugs used to control ADHD.

3. <http://www.mayoclinic.com>. See Diseases and Conditions, ADHD, in Children, References, DS00275. Page now discontinued.

4. Ibid.

5. <www.chadd.org/Content/CHADD/ "Understanding AD/HD : Causes." CHADD stands for "Children and Adults with Attention Deficit/ Hyperactivity Disorder." Accessed 11-16-10.

6. <http://health.nytimes.com/health/guides/disease/attention-deficit-hyperactivity-disorder-adhd/overview.html? WT.z_gsac=1>.

7. *Focus on the Family* magazine 32:5, May 2008, 36.

8. National Institutes of Health, "Fetal Alcohol Spectrum Disorders," July 2007, 1.

9. See Diseases and Conditions, ADHD, in Children, References, DS00275. Page now discontinued

10. *Fetal Alcohol Syndrome: a Parent's Guide to Caring for a Child Diagnosed with FAS* (Winston-Salem, N.C.: Wake Forest University Health Sciences, 2004), 13, 17. Published as an online book at <http://www.otispregnancy.org>. See Resources: "Other Education Materials and Links" to open online book. (Accessed 11-16-10).

11. <http://www.mayoclinic.com>. See Diseases and Conditions, Oppositional Defiant Disorder (ODD): Risk factors. (Accessed 11-16-10).

12. "Parenting a Child with AD/HD," National Resource Center on AD/HD, a Program of CHADD. For more information, visit <http://www.chadd.org> and <www.help4adhd.org>.

13. "ADHD & Your Child," 8, 12.

14. <http://www.teenswithproblems.com/home_contract.html>.

15. Joan Callander, *Second Time Around: Help for Grandparents Who Raise Their Children's Kids* (Wilsonville, Oreg.: BookPartners, 1999), 49.

Chapter 6

1. Kentucky Cabinet for Health & Family Services, Adoption Glossary, 6.

2. National Council on Child Abuse & Family Violence. <http://www.nccafv.org/child.htm>.

3. <http://preventchildabuseny.org/aboutchildabuse.shtml>. Sodomy, for the record, is anal sexual intercourse of one male with another, or anal or oral sexual union with a member of the opposite sex. Sexual union with an animal is also called sodomy. Definitions adapted from *Compact American Medical Dictionary*, 1998.

4. <http://www.preventchildabuseny.org>.

5. National Council on Child Abuse & Family Violence, <http://www.nccafv.org/child.htm>.

6. <http://preventchildabuseny.org/paprevsex.shtml>.

7. <http://preventchildabuseny.org/aboutchildabuse.shtml>.

8. Ibid.

9. National Council on Child Abuse & Family Violence, <http://www.nccafv.org/child.htm>.

10. <http://preventchildabuseny.org/aboutus.shtml>.

11. <http://preventchildabuseny.org/carecsexual.shtml>.

12. Ibid.

13. National Council On Child Abuse And Family Violence. <http://www.nccafv.org/child.htm>.

14. <http://preventchildabuseny.org/carecsexual.shtml>.

15. "Tips for Parents," Prevent Child Abuse New York, <http://preventchildabuseny.org/paprevsex.shtml>.

16. Ibid.

17. Last three bullets are from <http://www.nccafv.org/child.htm>. The remainder of the bulleted list is from the following source, by Sharon Bryson.

18. Sharon Bryson (child abuse therapist in the Fayette County, Kentucky, court system and Director of Field Education for the masters in social work program at Asbury University, Wilmore, Kentucky), speaking at Wilmore Free Methodist Church, April 16, 2008.

Chapter 7

1. Casey Family Programs National Center for Resource Family Support, as reported at <http://fostersurvivor.netfirms.com/statistics.shtml>.

2. "Facts for Families," American Academy of Child & Adolescent Psychiatry, *Foster Care* 64, updated May 2005, 1, <http://www.aacap.org/cs/root/facts_for_families/foster_care>.

3. <http://www.fostersurvivor.netfirms.com/mainpage.shtml>.

4. Crystal Murray, interview with the author at Capitol Plaza hotel, Frankfort, Kentucky, July 6, 2006.

5. CPS Watch, Inc., as reported at <http://fostersurvivor.netfirms.com/statistics.shtml>.

6. "Foster Care," Wikipedia, <http://en.wikipedia.org/wiki/Foster_care>.

7. "Facts for Families," 2.

8. "Facts for Families," 1.

9. <http://www.childwelfare.gov/pubs//factsheets/foster.cfm#key>. Data obtained from Adoption and Foster Care Analysis and Reporting System (AFCARS).

10. Casey Family Programs National Center for Resource Family Support, as reported at <http://fostersurvivor.netfirms.com/statistics.shtml>.

11. Child Welfare League of America, "Quick Facts About Foster Care," 1, <http://www.cwla.org/printable/printpage.asp>.

12. "You Just Love 'Em, Honey," *Spotlight on the Family*, Raleigh, N.C., Methodist Home for Children, fall 2007, 2.

13. English writer Samuel Johnson described fosterage in his book *A Journey to the Western Isles of Scotland*, 1775, <http://en.wikipedia.org/wiki/Fosterage>.

14. Casey Family Programs National Center for Resource Family Support, <http://fostersurvivor.netfirms.com/statistics.shtml>.

15. National Association of Social Workers, <http://fostersurvivor.netfirms.com/statistics.shtml>.

Chapter 8

1. For more on enabling, see these links:
<http://www.egetgoing.com/drug_addiction/enabling.asp> <http://www.egetgoing.com/drug_addiction/enabling_feelings.asp> <http://www.egetgoing.com/drug_addiction/enabling_behavior.asp> <http://www.egetgoing.com/drug_addiction/changing_enabling_behavior.asp>

2. Gene Doyle, interview with the author at Mr. Doyle's office, March 20, 2007. All quotations from Mr. Doyle in this book are from that interview.

3. Thomas, *When Love Is Not Enough*, 28, 103.

Chapter 10

1. Generations United at <http://ipath.gu.org/Kinsh6261201.asp>.

Chapter 11

1. <http://www.usdoj.gov/dea/concern/marijuana.html>.

2. <http://www.theantidrug.com/advice/advice-marijuana-use.asp>; <http://www.usdoj.gov/dea/concern/paraphernaliafact.html>.

3. <http://www.theantidrug.com/ei/where_sold.asp?print=true>.

4. <http://www.kidshealth.org>.

5. <http://www.nida.nih.gov/infofacts/Clubdrugs.html>.

6. Ibid.

7. <http://www.starliterecovery.com/hallucinogens.asp>.

8. Ibid.

9. <http://www.nida.nih.gov/DrugPages/DrugsofAbuse.html>; <http://ncadi.samhsa.gov/govpubs/PHD861/>.

10. <http://www.nida.nih.gov/DrugPages/DrugsofAbuse.html>.

11. <http://www.mayoclinic.com>. See Diseases and Conditions: Drug Addiction, search for "inhalant abuse," "Inhalant abuse: Is your child at risk?" (Accessed 11-16-10).

12. For more information, see <http://www.theantidrug.com/ei/signs_symptoms.asp?print=true>; <http://www.4troubledteens.com/drug-use-behavor.html>.

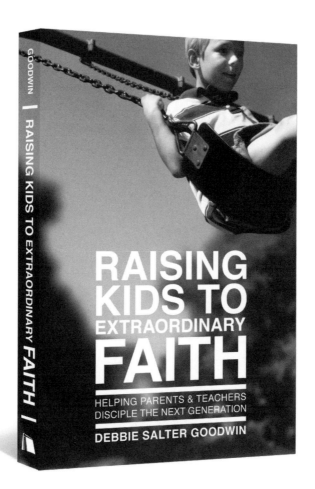

We want our children to know and love Jesus and learn what it means to be His disciple.

Filled with spiritual growth ideas and suggestions for developing faith-enriched homes and church environments, *Raising Kids to Extraordinary Faith* offers purposeful advice, spiritual insight, and essential awareness to help parents and ministry workers make discipleship the key component of their guidance.

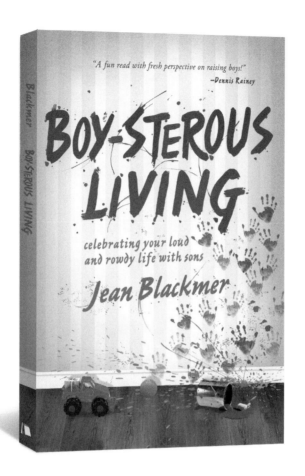

"A fun read with fresh perspective on raising boys!"
—Dennis Rainey

BOY-STEROUS LIVING

celebrating your loud and rowdy life with sons

Jean Blackmer

Celebrate your loud and rowdy life with sons.

Boy-sterous Living
ISBN 978-0-8341-2390-8

Available wherever books are sold.
www.BeaconHillBooks.com